BRIDGEWATER

CENTENNIAL CELEBRATION,

1856.

a

VIEW OF THE
OLD CHURCH AND TOWN-HOUSE,
near the centre of
ANCIENT BRIDGEWATER.

CELEBRATION

OF THE

Two-Hundredth Anniversary

OF THE

INCORPORATION OF BRIDGEWATER,

MASSACHUSETTS,

AT WEST BRIDGEWATER, JUNE 3, 1856;

INCLUDING THE

ADDRESS BY HON. EMORY WASHBURN, OF WORCESTER;

POEM BY JAMES REED, A.B., OF BOSTON;

AND THE OTHER EXERCISES OF THE OCCASION.

With an Appendix.

PUBLISHED BY REQUEST OF THE COMMITTEE OF ARRANGEMENTS.

BOSTON:
PRINTED BY JOHN WILSON AND SON,
22, SCHOOL STREET.
1856.

At a meeting of the Committee of Arrangements, held this day, the following vote was passed unanimously: —

Voted, That the thanks of the Committee be presented to the Hon. EMORY WASHBURN for his learned, eloquent, and interesting Address, delivered on the Two-Hundredth Anniversary of the Incorporation of the Town of ancient Bridgewater, and that he be requested to furnish us a copy thereof for the press.

A true copy. Attest,

FRANKLIN AMES, *Secretary*.

WEST BRIDGEWATER, June 5, 1856.

WORCESTER, June 20, 1856.

DEAR SIR,

The kind terms in which the Committee were pleased to communicate a request for a copy of the Address, which I had the honor to deliver on the third instant, hardly leave me free to deliberate. If it can be a means of gratifying any one, I do not feel at liberty to refuse it, and therefore hasten to comply with the wish expressed in this vote of the fifth instant.

I am, Sir,
Very respectfully your obedient servant,

EMORY WASHBURN.

FRANKLIN AMES, Esq., *Secretary*.

CONTENTS.

	PAGE.
INTRODUCTORY	9
OFFICERS AND COMMITTEES	11
ORDER OF PROCESSION	17
HYMN BY WILLIAM C. BRYANT, ESQ., OF NEW YORK	18
ADDRESS BY HON. EMORY WASHBURN, OF WORCESTER	20
POEM BY JAMES REED, A.B., OF BOSTON	83
HYMN BY REV. DANIEL HUNTINGTON, OF NEW LONDON	97
WELCOME ADDRESS BY HON. JOHN A. SHAW, OF BRIDGEWATER	99
REMARKS BY HON. EZEKIEL WHITMAN, OF EAST BRIDGEWATER	104
,, ,, HON. LEMUEL SHAW, OF BOSTON	110
,, ,, HON. EMORY WASHBURN, OF WORCESTER	116
,, ,, REV. RALPH SANGER, OF DOVER	118
,, ,, HON. GEORGE P. SANGER, OF BOSTON	121
,, ,, HON. WILLIAM BAYLIES, OF WEST BRIDGEWATER	124
,, ,, DR. EBENEZER ALDEN, OF RANDOLPH	126
,, ,, HON. AARON HOBART, OF EAST BRIDGEWATER	130
,, ,, HON. SETH SPRAGUE, OF DUXBURY	135
,, ,, HON. JAMES M. KEITH, OF ROXBURY	137

CONTENTS.

	PAGE.
SONGS WRITTEN BY MR. D. W. C. PACKARD, OF NORTH BRIDGEWATER	141
LETTER FROM HIS EXCELLENCY HENRY J. GARDNER	143
" " HON. EDWARD EVERETT, OF BOSTON	144
" " HON. CHARLES E. FORBES, OF NORTHAMPTON	144
" " HON. ISRAEL WASHBURN, JUN., OF MAINE	145
" " HON. ELIJAH HAYWARD, OF OHIO	146
" " HON. JAMES SAVAGE, OF BOSTON	148
" " HON. C. C. WASHBURN, OF WISCONSIN	149
ADDRESS TO THOSE WHO MAY CELEBRATE THE THIRD CENTENNIAL ANNIVERSARY	150

BRIDGEWATER

CENTENNIAL CELEBRATION.

A MEETING of citizens of the four Bridgewaters * was held at the Town-hall in West Bridgewater, Feb. 2, 1856, pursuant to public notice, to consider the expediency of celebrating the Second Centennial Anniversary of the Incorporation of the ancient town of Bridgewater, on the third day of June, 1856. Hon. JOHN A. SHAW, of Bridgewater, was chosen Chairman; and FRANKLIN AMES, Esq., of North Bridgewater, Secretary.

It was resolved unanimously to hold such a celebration at West Bridgewater, where the first white inhabitants of the old town settled; and a Committee of forty-eight was chosen, consisting of twelve persons from each of the Bridgewaters, to make all the arrangements therefor, and carry the same into exe-

---

* BRIDGEWATER was incorporated June 3, 1656.
NORTH BRIDGEWATER, June 15, 1821.
WEST BRIDGEWATER, February 16, 1822.
EAST BRIDGEWATER, June 14, 1823.

cution. Said Committee consisted of the following persons: —

Jonathan Copeland, Albe Howard, Pardon Copeland, Nahum Leonard, Nahum Snell, Thomas Ames, James Alger, Henry H. Whitman, Joseph Kingman, Austin Packard, Calvin Williams, and Dwelley Fobes, *of West Bridgewater.*

John A. Shaw, Artemas Hale, Philander Leach, Horace Ames, John Edson, Williams Latham, Thomas Cushman, David Perkins, Spencer Leonard, jun., Abram Washburn, Mitchell Hooper, and Calvin B. Pratt, *of Bridgewater.*

Welcome Young, William Allen, Azor Harris, James H. Mitchell, Samuel B. Allen, Benjamin W. Harris, Asa Mitchell, Aaron Hobart, jun., James Bates, Nathan Whitman, Seth Bryant, and Hector O. A. Orr, *of East Bridgewater.*

Eliab Whitman, Edward Southworth, jun., Perez Marshall, Franklin Ames, Ellis Packard, Martin L. Keith, George W. Bryant, Henry W. Robinson, Henry Howard, Isaac Kingman, Samuel Dunbar, and Jonas R. Perkins, *of North Bridgewater.*

It was decided by the Committee of Arrangements to have an address, a poem, and a dinner; and Austin Packard, Artemas Hale, William Allen, and Edward Southworth, jun., were chosen a Committee to procure suitable persons to deliver the address and poem, and to employ the services of such clergymen as they might think proper.

CENTENNIAL CELEBRATION. 11

Joseph Kingman, Calvin Williams, Henry H. Whitman, Mitchell Hooper, Williams Latham, Calvin B. Pratt, Benjamin W. Harris, James Bates, James H. Mitchell, Ellis Packard, Martin L. Keith, and George W. Bryant, were chosen a Committee to fix upon a definite plan of procedure, and report at the adjournment of the meeting.

In pursuance of the report of the last-named Committee, the following officers were chosen: —

President of the Day.

JOHN A. SHAW.

Vice-Presidents.

NAHUM LEONARD.	EZEKIEL WHITMAN.
JONATHAN COPELAND.	AARON HOBART.
BENJAMIN B. HOWARD.	WELCOME YOUNG.
WILLIAM BAYLIES.	CUSHING MITCHELL.
PARDON KEITH.	AZOR HARRIS.
ARTEMAS HALE.	ELIAB WHITMAN.
SAMUEL LEONARD.	SAMUEL DUNBAR.
PHILIP E. HILL.	JOSIAH W. KINGMAN.
HOLMES SPRAGUE.	EDWARD SOUTHWORTH.
SOLOMON ALDEN.	FRANKLIN AMES.

Treasurer.

AUSTIN PACKARD.

Chief Marshal.

AARON B. DRAKE.

Assistant Marshals.

THOMAS AMES.	JAMES BATES.
GEORGE L. ANDREWS.	FRANCIS M. FRENCH.

Toast-Master.

BENJAMIN W. HARRIS.

Assistant Toast-Masters.

JOSEPH KINGMAN.	GEORGE W. BRYANT.

DAVID PERKINS.

Committee of Finance.

DWELLEY FOBES.	NATHAN WHITMAN.
ROBERT PERKINS.	GEORGE W. BRYANT.

Committee on Sentiments, Invitations, and Reception of Guests.

AUSTIN PACKARD.	WILLIAM ALLEN.
JOSEPH KINGMAN.	ASA MITCHELL.
JOHN A. SHAW.	EDWARD SOUTHWORTH, jun.
ARTEMAS HALE.	JONAS R. PERKINS.

Committee on Music.

NAHUM SNELL.	EZRA KINGMAN.
SOLOMON KEITH.	ELLIS PACKARD.

Executive Committee.

THOMAS AMES.	WILLIAMS LATHAM.
HENRY H. WHITMAN.	CALVIN B. PRATT.
CALVIN WILLIAMS.	JAMES H. MITCHELL.
GEORGE WILBAR.	SETH BRYANT.
AMASA HOWARD.	ELLIS PACKARD.

MARTIN L. KEITH.

Committee to print the Address and Poem, with a Report of the Celebration.

AUSTIN PACKARD.	WILLIAM ALLEN.
ARTEMAS HALE.	FRANKLIN AMES.

Committee to prepare an Address to those who may celebrate the Third Centennial Anniversary.

JOSEPH KINGMAN.	WILLIAM ALLEN.
DWELLEY FOBES.	ASA MITCHELL.
JOHN A. SHAW.	EDWARD SOUTHWORTH, jun.
THOMAS CUSHMAN.	PAUL COUCH.

The Chief Marshal was authorized to appoint his aids, and the Assistant Marshals their aids.

The Executive Committee was authorized to act upon and decide all matters not specially assigned to any other Committee.

The several towns appropriated their proportion of one thousand dollars towards defraying the expenses of the celebration.

And the Committee on Printing was directed to enclose the various documents, relating to the Celebration, in a box, and deposit the same in the town-safe at Bridgewater, for the use of those who may celebrate the Third Centennial Anniversary.

The ringing of the bells on all the churches in the four towns, and the discharge of cannon, announced the dawn of the Centennial Day. The weather was as pleasant as could be desired, and a large number of people assembled to join in the festivities of the occasion.

Several places of historical note were appropriately designated, among which were the following: —

"CENTRE TREE."

A stone monument now occupies the place where the Centre Tree formerly stood. It was long known as the centre of Bridgewater, and was established, pursuant to an order of the Court at Plymouth, soon after the incorporation of the town. It is on the southerly side of the road between the railroad and the house of Thomas Hayward, who, with his ancestors, has owned and occupied the place about one hundred and fifty years.

"FLAT ROCK."

Rev. James Keith, the first minister of Bridgewater, is said to have preached his first sermon on this rock in 1664. An anecdote is related of him, the narration of which may help explain the meaning of a placard on the route of the procession. It appears that Minister Keith had a daughter, Mary, who gave her heart to Ephraim, son of John Howard, the first settler of that name. Mary's father did not approve of the match; notwithstanding which, the lovers were united. The displeased clergyman preached a sermon, appropriate to the occasion and to his feelings, from the following text: " Ephraim is joined to idols: let him alone." (Hos. iv. 17.) As time rolled on, Parson Keith became reconciled to his son-in-law, and learned to love and respect him. The parson then preached another sermon, and took for his text, " Is Ephraim my dear son? is he a pleasant child? For, since I spake against him, I do earnestly remember him still; therefore my bowels are troubled for him: I will surely have mercy upon him, saith the Lord." (Jer. xxxi. 20.)

"INDIANS HERE IMPOUNDED."

According to Mitchell's "History of Bridgewater," a number of Indian prisoners were conveyed into the Town Pound on the night of Aug. 3, 1676, and an Indian guard set over them. "They were treated with victuals and drink, and had a merry night; and the prisoners laughed as loud as the soldiers, not having been so well treated before for a long time."

The Green, selected as the place of general rendezvous, was admirably adapted to the purpose. It can be entered by five different roads; allowing a separate entrance for the procession from each of the four Bridgewaters, besides a common passage out when united in one column. Over each street through which the processions entered, was suspended one of the following inscriptions: —

"WEST PRECINCT."*
"SOUTH PRECINCT, 1716."
"EAST PRECINCT, 1723."
"NORTH PRECINCT, 1738."

Over the street through which the general procession passed from the Green, was erected a triumphal arch, surmounted by the American eagle and flags, with the inscription, —

"BRIDGEWATER, JUNE 3, 1656."

---

* The West Precinct, or Parish, was never incorporated by any act of the legislature, but succeeded the old town in the transaction of parochial affairs. — The figures show when the other parishes were incorporated.

In the centre of the Green, a flag-staff was erected, and a structure for the exhibition of antiquities. This is the place where stood the old meeting-house built in 1731, and which, for many years, served the double purpose of a church and town-house.

The houses of Jarvis D. Burrell, Daniel Chaplin, Isaac Howard, Jonas Leonard, and the store of Baker and Williams, fronting the Green, and the houses of Francis Perkins, Seneca Folsom, Thomas Ames, Benjamin Howard, Daniel H. Baker, and others, were elegantly and tastefully decorated, under the direction of Col. William Beals, of Boston.

The inhabitants of each town assembled at an early hour, at a short distance from the Green, and formed a procession in such order as their respective Marshals directed.

The general procession, which was one of the great features of the day, was formed on the Green, at ten o'clock in the morning, and marched under the arch, by the mills, the houses of Benjamin Howard, Daniel H. Baker, and the meeting-house, under the direction of the Chief Marshal, escorted by the North Bridgewater Light Dragoons, Capt. H. A. Raymond, and Gilmore's Salem Brass Band, occupying about forty minutes in passing a given point, in the following order: * —

---

* The procession was amused in passing by W. C. Bailey, who was beating and swingling flax.

CENTENNIAL CELEBRATION.

Aid.   CHIEF MARSHAL.   *Aid.*

PRESIDENT AND ORATOR OF THE DAY.

POET AND CHAPLAINS.

INVITED GUESTS.

CLERGYMEN OF THE FOUR BRIDGEWATERS.

COMMITTEE OF ARRANGEMENTS.

VICE-PRESIDENTS OF THE DAY.

Aid.   ASSISTANT MARSHAL.   *Aid.*

THE WEST-BRIDGEWATER PROCESSION,

Preceded by Flagg's Cornet Band,

Consisted of a large number of Citizens, with Banners, and the Pupils of the Public Schools, with their Teachers.

Aid.   ASSISTANT MARSHAL.   *Aid.*

THE BRIDGEWATER PROCESSION,

Preceded by the Boston Brass Band,

Had two beautifully painted Banners; one representing Bridgewater in 1656, the other in 1856. Accompanying the same procession was a large Carriage, containing a Representation of a School in Old Times, with the Teacher and her Pupils in the dress of those days. A gentleman rode on horseback, with a lady sitting on a pillion behind him. Then came a Carriage laden with Old and Modern Implements of Agriculture, followed by Old Chaises and other vehicles, filled with people dressed in the costume of former years.

Aid.   ASSISTANT MARSHAL.   *Aid.*

THE EAST-BRIDGEWATER PROCESSION,

Preceded by the Boston Brigade Band,

Comprised a Cavalcade of Citizens; a Corps of the Veterans of 1812, commanded by Capt. ELY BLANCHARD; a Representation of the Purchase of Bridgewater, in 1649, by Miles Standish, Samuel Nash, and Constant Southworth, — in behalf of the townsmen of Duxbury, and in the garb of our Puritan ancestors, — of Massasoit (or "Ousamequin," as he was then called), in the perfect costume of his tribe, from the feathery ornaments of the head to the decorated moccasons of the feet, with one hand resting upon a gun, and holding in the other the deed or written instrument of bargain and sale. The Scholars of the District Schools rode in carriages, covered with green boughs, bearing a Banner, inscribed with, — "We revere our Forefathers." Another Banner bore the date of "1723," — the time when the East Parish was incorporated.

| *Aid.* | ASSISTANT MARSHAL. | *Aid.* |

THE NORTH-BRIDGEWATER PROCESSION,

Preceded by the Brass Band of that Town,

Comprised a Corps of Soldiers dressed in the military costume of the Continentals, commanded by Capt. JOHN BATTLES; the Campello Rangers, Capt. ZIBA KEITH; the Protector Engine Company, Capt. C. L. HAUTHAWAY, with their engine beautifully decorated, and drawn by four horses; after which came the Enterprise Engine Company in uniform, and a large number of Citizens.

At twelve o'clock, the general procession entered the Pavilion, erected for the purpose by R. M. YALE, of Boston, in a field on the easterly side of the main street, between the houses of Azel Howard and William Copeland.

The exercises commenced by an Invocation by Rev. JONAS PERKINS, of Braintree.

The following Hymn, written by WILLIAM C. BRYANT, Esq., of New York, was sung by the assembled multitude to the tune of "Auld Lang Syne:"—

> Two hundred times has June renewed
>   Her roses, since the day
> When here, amid the lonely wood,
>   Our fathers met to pray.

> Beside this gentle stream, that strayed
>   Through pathless deserts then,
> The calm, heroic women prayed,
>   And grave, undaunted men.

Hymns on the ancient silence broke
    From hearts that faltered not,
And undissembling lips that spoke
    The free and guileless thought.

They prayed, and thanked the Mighty One
    Who made their hearts so strong,
And led them towards the setting sun,
    Beyond the reach of wrong.

For them he made that desert-place
    A pleasant heritage, —
The cradle of a free-born race
    From peaceful age to age.

The plant they set — a little vine —
    Hath stretched its boughs afar
To distant hills and streams that shine
    Beneath the evening star.

Ours are their fields, — these fields that smile
    With summer's early flowers:
Oh, let their fearless scorn of guile,
    And love of truth, be ours!

Prayer was offered by Rev. PAUL COUCH, of North Bridgewater.

Hon. EMORY WASHBURN, of Worcester, delivered the following Address: —

ADDRESS.

We have come up hither, to-day, to lay the offerings of cherished memories and honest pride upon altars which our fathers reared here in years that are past.

Two centuries have consecrated the spot by its history and associations; and we dedicate the day to the reminiscences which this anniversary is calculated to awaken.

Though there be little in the annals of such a community that might be deemed worthy of a place in a nation's history, it is because the same courage and fortitude, the same love of country, and the same devotion to truth and humanity, which have immortalized heroes and martyrs and patriots on a broader stage of action, have here been circumscribed within a narrower sphere.

Though the history of this little community may properly form the theme of our reflections on an anniversary like this, we can neither contemplate the characters of its founders, nor the events that led to the planting of this offshoot from the original colony, without recalling the men and the circumstances by which that colony itself was planted.

It cannot, however, be necessary, before this audience, to tell who and what were the Pilgrims who founded the Plymouth colony.

You know them; the world knows them; and their names will not perish till this wide continent itself shall have passed away. And standing, as we do, upon a spot which was witness to some of their struggles, and whose occupancy was among the early fruits of their triumph over the difficulties that surrounded them, the memory goes back instinctively to that train of events which was crowned by the planting of a colony of free and enlightened Englishmen on the shores of New England.

Bear with me, therefore, while I attempt to recall some of the circumstances which were connected with that system of training, and that sequence of events, which, in the order of Providence, made the founders of Plymouth the instruments of a social and political revolution more important in its consequences than any other that the world ever witnessed.

The world had, for centuries, exhibited the social antagonism of weakness and endurance on the part of the masses, and of arrogance and oppression on the part of their rulers, relieved, occasionally only, by the rise of some little republic, or the violent overthrow of some ancient dynasty.

But neither in the political condition of the nations of the Old World, nor the extent of knowledge diffused among the masses, was there any well-grounded hope of any thing like a radical reform. Old notions, old habits, old prejudices, and old institutions, had obtained such possession of the popular mind in the Old World, that, to human calculation, it seemed impossible to lift the weight that was pressing it down.

If the light at any time dawned on any favored spot, every ray was soon absorbed and extinguished by the thick and impenetrable darkness by which it was surrounded; and the world had for a long time waited for some great movement to arouse the masses to something like a common purpose, when the Reformation broke the spell which bigotry and superstition had thrown over the human mind.

But there was danger that even this great movement would exhaust itself and subside. The excitement arising from the novelty of its views had passed away; the force of old habits and associations was already beginning to be manifested in a returning attachment to forms, and a growing reverence for the pomp and ceremony of a ritual that had so long dazzled the senses of a superstitious multitude.

The leading spirits in that revolution had, one after the other, gone to their reward. Wickliff and Huss and Luther and Zwingli and Knox and Calvin had each done a noble work towards the religious emancipation of Christendom; but the spirit of trade and commerce, the love of ease and the possession of power, had begun to distract the counsels and subdue the zeal of those to whom had been intrusted the completion of the work. Even in England, the stronghold of the Reformation, the punctilios of ceremony, the vestments of the clergy, and the ritual of the church, had usurped that place in the public mind which the true spirit of Protestantism had assigned only to the truths and mysteries of our holy religion.

Between the intolerance of the Roman pontiff and the scarcely less intolerant catholicism of the head of the Protestant English church, Protestantism was in danger of being crushed for ever. Power was against it; the passions of the human heart were against it; worldly ambition was against it; and the traditions of the past, as well as the love of present ease and comfort, were against it; and in few spots in the Old World was there any thing like a free play of the human reason to be found.

As we now look at the subject, from this point of view, one place of refuge only presents itself, where the faith of the reformers may be safe; and that is the untrodden wilderness of the New World. There, away from the seductions of worldly power and worldly honors, beyond the empire of fashion and of rituals, with a field open and free for culture, Truth may strike its roots deep into a friendly soil, and spring up in vigor and beauty to bear the fruit of free institutions.

But place was not the only circumstance concerned in the preservation and development of great principles like those of the Reformation. Nor was it mere freedom in matters of conscience to which that movement tended. Though it came in the form of independence in religious opinions, its scope embraced civil as well as religious liberty, and depended for its ultimate success upon the character of its actors, and the opportunity they enjoyed for the exercise of the powers they possessed.

And, as we contemplate this subject more in detail, we perceive, that, in order to plant a colony which should stand by its own strength, and grow by its own inherent energy, it must be made of sterner stuff, and be actuated by higher motives, than any that had hitherto been attempted in the northern parts of America.

Enterprise after enterprise had failed, although fostered and encouraged by royal favor or the patronage of the great. Cartier and Roberval had abandoned their efforts to colonize Canada, while sustained by the prestige and the power of the monarch of France. The settlers at Sagadahoc, though patronized and encouraged by Popham, the Lord Chief Justice of England, after the experience of a single winter, had gone back to England, defeated and disheartened. Gosnold, under the favor of the Earl of Southampton, had begun an experiment, which, after a few months, he had ingloriously given up, even before he had encountered the rigors of the climate or the discomforts of the emigrant.

Smith had explored, and given the attractive name of " New England" to, this portion of the continent; but the men who should plant it, who should open its rugged soil to the sun, and fit it for the habitations of civilized life, were yet to be found. If they were not yet to be created, they had not yet been educated or trained for such a work as this. There were for the work certain qualifications which were essential to success; and even these, without a proper course of training, would be found inadequate for its accomplishment.

Nor are we at a loss to judge from what nation, and from what race, the founders of such a colony must come.

For centuries, the Briton, the Roman, the Saxon, and the Norman, had been mingling and blending into what we call the Anglo-Saxon race, the traits of whose character are still being manifested in the onward march towards universal empire. If we analyze that character, it will be found to embrace the very elements the most needed in a work like that which we now know the founders of Plymouth colony had before them.

Promptness in devising plans, combined with a dogged perseverance in their execution; calmness in judgment, kept in vigorous action by the stimulus of self-love, and ambition for power, — were some of the characteristics of that race, whose political wisdom, inexhaustible resources, and warlike prowess, have filled so important a page in the history of nations.

But something more even than this was wanted. These national traits of character required to be warmed into enthusiasm. It wanted that that spark of liberty, which, though but a spark, had been kept alive from the time of the old Saxon heptarchy, should be fanned into a flame, till every part of the body politic should be warmed and animated with a common and generous glow of sympathy.

The Reformation had done much to awaken this train of thought and feeling. But it remained for the Puritans of England to accomplish what the Reformation had begun.

To their eye, earthly honors were as nothing to the crown of glory that awaited them beyond the grave; and the world's treasures were poor in the light of that inheritance which awaited the saints who should persevere to the end. They read, in their Bibles, of the common origin and common destiny of their race; and they stood up erect before thrones and rulers, spurning alike the civil despot, and the tyranny of the hierarch that denied to them the pure and simple worship which their hearts craved and their consciences dictated.

Nor was this all that was needed to establish a community, without a charter to unite or royal bounty to foster it, — a colony planted in the desert, and left to pitiless storms and scorching suns, to thrive, if at all, by its own vital, seminal principle.

For such a community, there must be a singleness of purpose, a homogeneity of character and views and feelings, amongst its members, rarely, if ever, before attained by any considerable body of men. Without these, their union would be like the sands upon which it was to be planted, — scattered by the first gust of dissension, and swept away by the first storm that fell upon it.

The process by which this state of feeling was to be attained was, like all the great measures of Providence, simple, and, in the end, clear and intelligible.

With England as it then was, the idea of bringing the minds of men in different parts of the kingdom into sufficient harmony to carry forward such an enterprise would have been little better than an idle dream. The historians of England have told us of the condition of that country at that time. They had no means of creating, or keeping alive, a public sentiment. Books were scarce and costly, and read by comparatively few. Newspapers they had none; and even the intercourse by post was only along a few principal lines of communication, in its slow progress, and at infrequent periods. And York was scarcely nearer to London than we are; and Devonshire and Lincoln were, as communities, as much strangers to each other as Edinburgh is now to Paris or Ostend.

Where, then, are we to look for such a community as should furnish the school in which to train the men and women who were to plant New England?

Bear in mind, that to do this required them to go forth into the wilderness, to give up the comforts of civilized life, and that they are there to rear a Christian commonwealth, without any guide or chart to direct them save the dictates of conscience and an enlightened common sense. And we may readily perceive that the place for training such men is not amongst the luxuries of the city, the busy haunts of trade or commerce; but away from these, among the rural homes of England, and removed, as far as might be, from the parasites of power.

And as we recall the history of the men, who, in fact, founded Plymouth, we find that it was in precisely such a region as this that God in his providence gathered that little church, under Robinson and Brewster, which was to form the nucleus of a mighty nation of freemen.

Upon the confines of Nottingham, York, and Lincoln, amidst a population purely agricultural, within the Hundred of Basset-Lawe, lay the little village of Scrooby. So obscure has it been, and so little known to history, that its very name, till recently, had well-nigh been forgotten. Yet there, within that sequestered village, did that little band of Separatists come together to worship God, and keep alive each other's faith and courage. Its name can scarcely be deciphered on the map of England. The manor-house in which Brewster dwelt, and within which they met, has long since disappeared. The traveller, for two hundred years, has passed by the spot, unconscious that it possessed any thing of historical interest. Nor was it till a few years since, that the devoted zeal of an English antiquary for the memory of the Pilgrims traced up to this, its fountainhead, the little wellspring of the Plymouth colony.

But as we contemplate the spot, the men, the motive, and the result, we find that it needs no effort of the imagination, no conception of classic fable, to give dignity or interest to its story. It was there that the process of union and assimilation was begun; it was there that the men who were to form one homogeneous body, in order to achieve success, were trained in the school of adversity. The tie that bound them was the sympathy of a common nature, animated by a common hope, involved in a common destiny, and kept in harmonious action by the pressure of a common danger.

But though the men had been found; though, amidst the dangers by which they were surrounded, a place of comparative safety had been provided for meeting and for counsel, — the time for action had not yet arrived. Some more searching test of courage and fidelity was yet to be applied. And the next step in the sequence of events was their act of self-banishment. They were at last forced to fly from the fire of persecution which was besetting them on every side, and, in sorrow and desolation, sought a refuge, from the ruthless ferocity of their own countrymen, upon the friendly shores of Protestant, prosperous Holland.

This, it will be remembered, was in the year 1608.

Were we to stop here, and, ignorant of the fate of these fugitives from their homes, were we now to open the page of history for the first time, should we not expect to read how that little band, one after the other, were swallowed up in the populous sea into which they had thrown themselves? Trade, commerce, prosperous industry, worldly ease, and an untrammelled exercise of their own forms of worship, were busy in quenching that fire of enthusiasm which nerved them to meet a hostile persecution.

Their children must grow up among strangers, and gradually lose their mother tongue, till, by every law of human calculation, long before even the first century had closed over that community of English Protestants and Separatists, they had been merged into respectable, prosperous, nationalized men of Holland.

But, if we open that volume of history at the end of eleven years, we find that they have indeed passed through this ordeal, — ten times more trying than the fines and stripes and prisons from which they had escaped in England; and they have come out unscathed. They have been tried by the temptations and fascinations of the world; but they are the same little church, not of the lonely rural hamlet of Scrooby, but the worldly, populous city of Leyden. And Robinson is there; and Winslow has joined them; and Bradford is working at his trade there; and Brewster is there to keep alive the spirit which had animated them when his roof was their only shelter. But they saw the dangers that surrounded them as we now see them, — the dangers of that very safety and prosperity which they had sought by flight; and they were ready to go forth again, into the only refuge which was left for them, — the wilderness of America.

There they may build their own altars, and worship in their own language; there may they rear their children, away from the world's delusive temptations, and hope, that, when they shall be gathered to their fathers, the faith for which they have suffered will still be kept pure in the sanctuary of a free church.

But, though thus trained by this long discipline, there was yet one more step in the process of preparation to be taken, before their final exodus. In the language of a writer of that day, " the wheat had yet to be winnowed," that none but the sound and ripe and fitting grain should be employed to plant the virgin soil of New England.

Let us bear in mind, that, though unconsciously to themselves, those who were to engage in that enterprise were to constitute a Body Politic, as well as a Christian church, in the management of whose affairs qualities of a high and varied character were to be required. Mere piety, and a spirit of devotion, were not enough. They were to encounter danger; and they needed the heroism as well as the trained valor of the soldier. They were to frame and administer a form of government, till then new and untried; and they must have political sagacity, legislative wisdom, and executive talent. The forest was to be subdued, a hardy soil to be brought into cultivation, and the bays and shallows of the ocean to be sounded by the lines of the fisherman; and they must have rugged hands for toil, as well as wise heads for counsel. And, above all, they needed that which gave to their English homes their chief charm, to sustain their courage, and to cheer them in their labors, — the untiring devotion, the kind assiduities, and the hopeful fortitude of woman; and, without these, they would have failed, as other colonies had done before them.

I pass over the sad parting at Delft Haven. I stop not to speak of the "Speedwell," abandoned, at last, as hopelessly unseaworthy. I follow the track of the lonely "Mayflower," freighted, as she is, with the destinies of this Western World. I look in upon her crowded cabin, as she goes pitching and laboring on in her solitary way across the stormy ocean; and, at length, I listen to the voice of thanksgiving that goes up from the patient, tempest-tost, betrayed, yet hopeful group that crowd her deck, as they look out for the first time upon the sands of Cape Cod, on the 11th of November, 1620. And, regarding them in the unerring light of history, let me ask, if, among that hundred souls, there be not the very elements that are requisite to accomplish the work they have undertaken? Which of these are wanting?

There is the pious Brewster, still true and faithful to his little flock; there is the brave old Carver, and there the wise and prudent Bradford, the accomplished and courteous Winslow, and the gallant, chivalrous Standish. And there, too, is the sobered matron, with a mother's cares; the young and hopeful wife, and the blushing maiden. And there are White and Allerton and Alden and Warren, and those other names that have become household words in these homes of the Pilgrims. They are all there; and, as you look over that roll, tell me, is not the work in which Providence has been engaged, through the changes and revolutions of more than a century, about to be consummated? The tried men have been found at last; the ties that bound them to Old England have been severed; and the ship that bore them from her shores has let go her anchor upon the soil of New England.

The value of that disciplinary training through

which they had passed was tested before they had even set foot upon that soil. They found themselves beyond the limits of their charter, and, without a government, thrown homeless on a wintry coast, beyond the reach or the protection of any law.

But not a murmur is heard, not a thought of license or insubordination is cherished. Unknown to them, Providence had designed, through them, to demonstrate the capacity of man for self-government; and, in the very cabin of the "Mayflower," that solemn, memorable compact was entered into, which stands out upon the page of history as the first free civil compact of government that the world had ever witnessed.

Brief, however, as is that paper, and simple and earnest as is its language, how noble was its conception! — the germ of a free, democratic State, the first development of that grand idea of political equality which has spread out over this vast continent its busy, prosperous millions of freemen, and has been moving the nations of Europe as with an earthquake's power.

But, in attempting to do justice to history, let me not do injustice to the true grandeur of the Pilgrim character. No one pretends they came here to proclaim an abstract theory of government, or to record their names upon a roll of parchment, in the fanciful hope of their being read by coming generations. They came here for other and different purposes;

and the adoption of the framework of civil government in the harbor of Cape Cod was but one of the series of acts and events which illustrate what I have so often repeated, — the perfection of that discipline to which they had been subjected. No emergency found them unprepared; no vicissitude of fortune discomforted or disturbed them. It was the promptitude of the accomplished general, never surprised, never off his guard, and coolly meeting, amidst the very din of battle, the shifting and changing fortunes of the day. It was the practised eye and quick intelligence of the experienced helmsman in the storm, the calm self-possession and keen sagacity of the wise statesman when the affairs of state press most heavily upon him.

But, in the case of the Pilgrims, instead of submitting, as a body, to the guidance and control of some master-spirit, each felt a share of a common responsibility, and submitted his own will to that of the whole body; so that, whatever measures they adopted, they were the result of the combined judgment and good sense of the whole number. And, in this way, they not only planted a free church in a free state, but developed the germ of that New-England — may I not say *Yankee?* — character, which, in its vitalizing influence, was felt in every colony and town and household that grew up on its rugged soil, — that character, which, in the long struggle with the mother country in after-years, so often supplied the place of an organized government; providing in their destitution the sinews of war, and crowning the work at last with a free constitution.

But I am anticipating.

The adoption of this simple form of government was completed by the election of Carver as their governor; and, without misgiving or delay, they set about selecting a place for the seat of their little commonwealth. And here, again, the hand of Providence was manifest, in having thrown them upon a part of the coast which a pestilence had nearly depopulated, leaving it literally vacant for the occupation of the new-comers.

After one month's exploration, urged on by the rapid approach of winter, — for snow had already begun to fall, — they discovered a spot which the historian informs us " they supposed fit for situation: at least, it was the best they could find; and the season and their present necessity made them glad to accept it." That spot has become the shrine to which the modern pilgrim turns his footstep; and " Forefathers' Day " is the holiest in New England's calendar.

Will it be said that I have dwelt too long upon the character of the men and women who braved the horrors of that first dreadful winter, and literally made that spot holy ground by the prayers with which it was consecrated, and the memory of the dead whose ashes were mingled with its till then unbroken soil? There is nothing alien or far-fetched in the sketch, if we apply it to the character of the founders of Bridgewater. If none of the " first-comers " actually removed to this spot, three of them were among the original men of Duxbury to whom the township was granted. Three of the thirty-five who came in the " Fortune," the first vessel that arrived after the departure of the " Mayflower," are found among these proprietors; and one who came in the third vessel, the " Anne," in 1623. So that the founders of Bridgewater were so far associated and identified with the " old-comers," or " forefathers " of the colony, that, in speaking of the characteristics of the one, we, in effect, are but doing justice to the other. Many of them, moreover, are supposed to have come over from Leyden within the first ten years of the colony; and when, at last, they settled this frontier plantation, they did little more than transfer to a new locality the wisdom they had been taught in the rugged experience through which they had passed, the love of civil and spiritual liberty which had exiled them from their English homes, and the laws and infant institutions which had grown out of their condition as colonists.

We, therefore, cannot do justice to them or the occasion, without referring to some of the measures of government and police which the founders of the colony adopted for the promotion of its interests. There is a spirit, pervading them all, which seems never to have been lost sight of; and that is the personal security, the equal protection, and the practical independence, of those who were admitted to the rights of freemen. Their rulers were elected by a popular vote. The whole body of freemen, for eighteen years, united in making their own laws, and, at last, only substituted delegates elected for the purpose because they had become too numerous to act collectively.

The laws they enacted, though we may smile at some of them, cannot now be read without pride and admiration. The true character of their early legislation and institutions will be better appreciated when the work of publication shall be accomplished in which such able hands are now employed, which is to place within the reach of every one a complete record of the Plymouth and Massachusetts colonies. But it would more than serve my purpose, if I could take that volume, known as the "Plymouth Laws," which was published by our Legislature in 1836, and present them, one by one, to your attention. I would ask you to remark their fitness for the condition under which the colonists found themselves, to what extent they borrowed some of the best provisions of law under which they had been bred, and with what wisdom and foresight they laid deep the foundations of a free State. It should be remembered, that the first satisfactory charter they had been able to obtain was in 1629. At that time, in the language of that charter, " by the special providence of God, and their extraordinary care and industry, they had increased their plantation to near three hundred people; and were, on occasions, able to relieve any planters, or others of his majesty's subjects, who might fall upon that coast."

During this period, the compact of the "Mayflower" had been the basis of their popular form of government; but they never seem to have forgot that which was due to the character and self-respect of freemen. The settlement of Plymouth, in the cant phrase of the present day, was an exercise of "squatter sovereignty" which needs no popular harangue or partisan press to dignify or defend. It was to create a new home for freedom; it was to plant on that soil institutions whose growth should root out and overtop every baleful parasite like Slavery, that weakens and wastes the stock upon which it fastens and feeds.

I open, then, that volume; and the first legislative act on which the eye rests is "that criminal facts, and all matters of trespasses and debts between man and man, shall be tried by twelve honest men, impanelled by authority, in form of a jury, upon their oaths." When we remember with what tenacity the people of England had always clung to this relic of Saxon liberty, through all the vicissitudes of tyranny and oppression through which they had passed, trial by jury cannot, indeed, be claimed as a new discovery in political science. But that it should be so early declared, and be made, as it were, one of the very foundation-stones of their political fabric, serves to show, that, next to their duty to God, the duty of guarding the rights of their fellow-men lay nearest their hearts.

Of some of their laws, indeed, the progress of the age has superseded the necessity. And when we recall the scramble there is for office, high or low, and how greatly the number of candidates exceed the places that are to be filled, we may be pardoned a smile when we read, " *If, now or hereafter, any are elected to the office of governor, and will not stand to the election, nor hold nor execute the office for his year, that then he shall be amerced in twenty pounds fine.*"

Alas! how empty would be that treasury, in our day, that had no other source of supply than the fines that should be paid by those who " will not stand to the election," be the office what it may! Unfortunately for the profit of the thing, our modern Carvers and Bradfords need no such stimulus to their patriotism as a penalty of twenty pounds for refusing to serve their country.

I might, if time permitted, ask you to look at the laws they enacted for the management of the economical interests of the colony, — the maintenance of highways as a public charge, the establishment of public registries of deeds, and various other measures, which have become so familiar from use that we forget the credit which is due to the wisdom that devised them.

Were we to pursue our investigations, we might discover how early that system of legislation began to be adopted, which seeks, by penal enactments, to extirpate bad personal habits, while the tastes and passions and propensities that generate these habits are in their full vigor.

Among these is one against the " great abuse of taking tobacco, in a very uncivil manner, openly in the town-streets, and as men pass upon the highways, and also in the fields, or as men are at work in the woods and fields, to the neglect of their labors, and *the great reproach of this government.*" But I greatly fear that this " Maine Law " against a filthy habit soon fell dead upon the statute-book; and that the world will go on smoking, in defiance alike of royal counterblasts and Puritan legislation, of soiled carpets and domestic discomfort.

There is another class of laws standing upon the statute-book of Plymouth colony, which, in justice to the men of that day, ought not to be passed over in silence; and that is the laws under which what are there called " Quaker Ranters or other notoriouse heritiques," including such men as Lyford and Oldham, found so cold a reception, and so determined a resolution to exclude them from the colony.

That this should have been done by the very men who had dared every thing, and endured all things, for the free exercise of conscience, has been regarded as a most culpable and inexcusable inconsistency of conduct. But, in this, we are in danger of doing them gross injustice. That they had been born before the light of religious tolerance had been shed upon the nations, was their misfortune, it may be; and that they were born with human passions and weaknesses, as they were with human forms, may detract from their claims upon the respect of others. But wherein, after all, consists the ground of censure and reproach, that men, who had gone so far and suffered so much to find a place where they should be free from intrusion and outside annoyance, should have felt disturbed and angry to be followed, and jostled in the very sanctuary of their own homes, by men who had done nothing to aid them, and felt no sympathy with them, in faith or taste, or desire for the advancement of the colony?

It was to them like the intrusion of an unwelcome visitor into one's family circle, who comes to cavil and find fault, to call the master hard names, and plague and pester the inmates by rude deportment and bad manners. It is fashionable to call this *intolerance* and *persecution*; and, much as we may lament the ignorance and folly that sought by such means to keep out heresy and schism, we should, I apprehend, ascertain, if we pursued the inquiry, that there was much less of a spirit of persecution in these measures of government, than of a desire and determination to be let alone themselves.

But, pleasant as it would be to dwell upon the history of the social and political condition of the colony, in which many connected with the early history of Bridgewater took a part, time compels me to forego the one, while I briefly call your attention to the other.

For twelve years after the settlement of Plymouth, the colony contained but a single town. Duxbury was formed into a church and town in 1632, and was followed by Scituate in 1636. Bridgewater formed the tenth, in order of time, of these little bodies politic into which the colony was divided.

I can scarcely refer to one circumstance, in the organization of the colonies of New England, which exerted so marked and lasting an influence upon their prosperity, their strength, and their ultimate success, as the subdivision of their territory into townships, and the creation of these into corporate bodies for municipal purposes.

I know not to what happy thought, or to what circumstance in their experience, we owe this then novel arrangement of the parts in relation to the whole. It was not probably so much the result of any particular foresight, as of that ready tact and excellent common sense which so often guided them in the measures they adopted. Originally identified with their church organizations, each of these corporations became actors in the political as well as the spiritual affairs of the colony; while to their charge was committed much of the management of its economical concerns.

Through these, bodies of citizens were frequently brought together to confer with each other, and to discuss topics of a common interest, till a common sentiment was created; and the interests of these, collectively, went to make up very much of that which we call the commonwealth. The effect of this is seen in the universal readiness with which the people of New England engage in the discussion of popular questions in popular debates, which travellers amongst us have so often admired. But it enters no less decidedly into the business of government. Each of these little republics exercises a governmental control within itself, independent of that of the state, though altogether in harmony with it. And when, at the final rupture of the province with the mother country, the organized government of the whole body politic became extinct, civil order was maintained, moneys were raised, the trainbands organized and sent into the field, and the scenes of Lexington and Bunker Hill enacted, by the combined action of the citizens of independent towns.

Nor is it in their political influence alone that these little democracies act so important a part in our social organization: they supply one of the strong ties of local association and attachment that bind the citizen to his country. It is something more than country; it is something more even than home. It is not merely the hill that looked so tall to us in our childhood, nor the tree beneath whose shade we played, nor the old familiar schoolhouse in which we first carved the rude initials of our names, that bind us so strongly, in after-days, to that magic circle within which were clustered what go to make up our earliest home. These are all associated in our memory with the name and history of some town or village, till it becomes a part of our very selves. Men may tell us that these are "bodies corporate," and that, in the eye of the law, they have neither souls to animate nor hearts to feel. But when the dust of a parent has been mingled with its soil; when the grass on some little mound, where we have laid away the richest of the heart's treasures, has been moistened by the tears of affection, — the man is unworthy of the form he wears whose soul is not knit with a tie of holy communion with every spot and scene and old familiar name which go to make up that physical and moral and social entity, the town, where he was born, or in whose prosperity he has shared in the struggles and successes of middle life.

The first grant of the plantation, afterwards incorporated into the town of Bridgewater, was made by the colony to Duxbury, as a compensation for the loss of territory occasioned by the creation of Marshfield into a township in 1645.

It embraced a territory of eight miles square, but was afterwards increased to ninety-six square miles; but, like similar grants from the court, it was in the nature of a pre-emption right, whereby the grantees became authorized to acquire the title to the soil from the native proprietors. In accordance with this principle, a committee of the grantees, consisting of Miles Standish, Samuel Nash, many years sheriff of the colony, and Constant Southworth, whose mother had married Governor Bradford, was appointed to obtain the requisite title-deeds from the good old Massasoit, within whose jurisdiction this territory was situated. The very names of this committee are a sufficient guaranty of honorable and fair dealing on the part of the purchasers; and we find, among the muniments of their title, a deed of the date of 1649, bearing the handmark of that constant and early friend of the white man, under the name of Ousamequin.

Tradition points out the spot where this act of purchase was completed, which once bore the name of "Sachem's Rock."* But it is sad to think, that, of all that race who then peopled this region, nothing but tradition now remains. It is sad to recall in how short a time not a drop of the blood of the Sachem of Pokanoket, whose hand of friendship welcomed our fathers to these shores, was to be found in the veins of any living being.

True, it was a long and bloody struggle that closed the tragic history of his race. Scarce a vestige of the homes of his warriors can now be traced; and save

---

* It is situated in what is now East Bridgewater, and still bears the name of "Sachem's Rock."

some such uncouth memorial as is appended to the deed of these lands, or is now and then turned up by the furrow in some rude implement of husbandry or savage warfare, nothing remains to tell us of the once-powerful tribe that fished in these streams, and hunted in these forests, and lit their council-fires around these scenes of prosperous industry and thrift.

> "The red men have passed,
> Like the strewn leaves of autumn dispersed by the blast."

But, to the honor of the founders of Bridgewater, a disposition to deal fairly with the aboriginal proprietors of the soil was ever manifested, so long as any claim remained to be adjusted. We find them, in 1686, raising a committee to "bargain, buy, and pay for any just interest" that Josiah Sachem had in the town of Bridgewater; which was soon after honorably and satisfactorily done. And it should be remembered, in this connection, that this was written a few years after the termination of Philip's war, in which, though the town suffered less in comparison than most of the frontier settlements, its inhabitants took a brave and active part; and, though the claim here set up was not by one of the Wampanoags, it was not always easy to discriminate, in the feelings of the sufferers, between the different members of a race who had carried on war in the same savage manner.

To the usual horrors of an Indian warfare, there had been united a courage and a determination on the part of the wily chief of Montaup,* and a wide-spread union of the tribes of New England, that threatened extermination to the white men. It had been literally a death-struggle of the two races. Nor can we, at this day, form any adequate conception of the constant apprehension under which the settlers of these towns had lived. No spot was safe. The very darkness of midnight was no shelter against the prowling savage. Even the church in which they worshipped was converted into a fortress, in 1675, by means of palisadoes, "for the safety of the town in the time of danger, to be made," says the record, "with half trees, seven feet above the ground, six rood long and nine rood wide, besides the flankers every quarter or squadron to doe each of them a side or an end;" and it was within such a shelter as this only that they had dared to meet even for the purpose of worshipping God.

From the few notices that remain of the part which the inhabitants took in that struggle with Philip, we may judge somewhat of its extent by the numbers who engaged in the active duty of soldiers. There were not, at that time, more than fifty persons capable of bearing arms in the town; and, from the remote-

---

* The mode of spelling the name of the seat of King Philip here adopted is believed to be that used by the Indians: the name, as commonly received, is "Mount Hope."

ness of the seaboard, we are told, " they were strongly urged to desert their dwellings, and repair to the towns by the seaside." But, so far from complying with this suggestion, we find seventeen of their number at one time hastening to the relief of Mattapoiset and the people of Swansey; and, on another occasion, twenty of their number encountering a much larger body of the enemy, and taking seventeen of them prisoners.

But, in the disposition of those prisoners, we are obliged to open a page in the history of the colony, over which it would be well for their memories if oblivion could draw a friendly veil. I have spoken of the general sense of justice with which the early colonists treated the native tribes around them; and we all know with what sorrow the good Robinson lamented that they " had not converted some before they had killed any " of these sons of the forest, when he heard of the deadly encounter between Standish and Pecksuot, the treacherous boaster of his strength and prowess, and in which the latter was slain.

But the circumstance to which I allude was the order of the court, in 1676, " that all such as had any Indian captive, above the age of fourteen years, should dispose of the same out of the colony by the first of the next December, on pain of forfeiting every such Indian or Indians to the use of the colony."

I would gladly record some decided disavowal of such a measure by the people of Bridgewater; but justice requires me to transcribe a vote of the 21st August, 1676, upon the question, "Who should have the money that was made of the Indians that were sold last?" alluding to the prisoners already mentioned, who had been taken by the Bridgewater soldiers, and had been sold at Plymouth by order of the court.

The record reads in these words: "And the vote passed, that the soldiers that took them should have the money. The contrary being called, I see but three men, at most, who hold up their hands to the contrary." It should be borne in mind, that the custom of enslaving captives taken in war was long regarded as an act of merciful commutation for the forfeiture of the life which they had incurred; and that it is difficult for us to measure the advance that has been made in the science of political morality between the sentiments which then universally prevailed, and the feeling of New England now, that denies the right of property in human beings. It may have been deemed a measure of necessity for the safety of the colonists, to dispose of those bold, fierce warriors beyond the possibility of return; and therefore it was that they sold them away into slavery. But, whatever might have been the feelings and sentiment of the General Court of the colony, I cheerfully accept, for the men of Bridgewater, the construction which has been put upon the vote which I have just quoted by one of her worthiest sons, who, amidst the honors he has received in another State, has never ceased to be sensitive to her honor,* that "this disposition of these prisoners was so repulsive to the feelings and obnoxious to the principles of the Bridgewater people, that they would not permit the money for which they were sold to come into the general treasury; and they voted 'that the soldiers that took them should have it.'"

And this view I am happy to find strengthened by the known and openly avowed opinions of their venerable pastor, Mr. Keith, who, to his honor be it remembered, when the question was submitted to the clergy of the colony what should be done with the wife and little son of Philip, who had been taken prisoners, strongly maintained the duty of exercising mercy, against the judgment of many of his clerical brethren. His feeling would have been to spare the little lad, then but nine years of age, from the life of slavery in Bermuda into which he was eventually sold.† I am the more confirmed in this favorable judgment of the views of the people of this town upon the subject of slavery, from the fact, that as late as 1754, when there were in the county of

---

* Hon. Elijah Hayward, of McConnelsville, Ohio, formerly Commissioner of the Land Office at Washington, Judge of the Supreme Court of Ohio, &c., — a lineal descendant, in the fifth degree, from Thomas Hayward, one of the earliest settlers in Bridgewater.

† The following extract from the letter of the Rev. Mr. Keith serves to show how the clergy of that day illustrated and tested questions of a politico-moral character: "I long to hear what becomes of Philip's wife and son. I know there is some difficulty in that Psalm cxxxvii. 8, 9; though I think it may be considered whether there be not some specialty and somewhat extraordinary in it. That law, Deut. xxiv. 16, compared with the commended example of Amaziah, 2 Chron. xxv. 4, doth sway much with me in the case under consideration."

Plymouth one hundred and thirty-three slaves, and in the whole province nearly five thousand, the statistics from which I have quoted do not show a single slave in Bridgewater! All honor to such abolition, that begins the work of discarding slavery, black or white, at home, and speaks so much more effectively by example than the cheap tribute of philippic and invective!

The settlement of the town was begun, on the part of the proprietors, in 1650, in the part now called West Bridgewater; though it seems that one family had come from Salem, and settled here, four years before that time. This was the well-known family of Edson, whose members, for so many years, took so leading a part in the affairs of the town and province. It was the first interior town settled in the colony; but it was not until the 3d June, 1656, that it was incorporated as such. This was done, in the briefest possible terms, by the simple order, " that henceforth Duxbury new plantation be allowed to be a township by itself, distinct from Duxbury, and to be called by the name of Bridgewater."* From that time, she took her place among the little bodies politic of Plymouth, until that colony was merged in her more powerful, and, as was sometimes thought, grasping neighbor. But whether we contemplate her history in its con-

---

* It nowhere appears, that I can learn, why this name was adopted rather than that of any other of the towns of Old England; though possibly some of its early settlers may have come from the English Bridgewater.

nection with that of the Old Colony, or of Massachusetts as a province, or as an independent commonwealth, we shall find that she has sustained her share of every public duty and burden, and has illustrated, in the character of her children, those public and domestic virtues which command respect, while they insure thrift and independence. It has therefore been with a just and honest pride, that her sons and her sons' sons, who are scattered all over the Union, have watched her progress, and felt that her honor was in no small degree identical with their own. And it is with such feelings that some of these have come back to-day, to revive old associations, and listen to the recital of some of the reminiscences which the recurrence of the day is calculated to awaken.

To more than one of these, I ought to express my acknowledgment for the aid I have received, even in the imperfect manner in which I am able to present the topics suitable for the occasion;* and, as I recall this, I am painfully reminded how much better justice would have been done to the subject in other hands, had I not yielded judgment to inclination, by following impulses awakened by the memory of an ancestry whose history is associated with that of this ancient town.

---

* Among these, I ought to mention Judge Hayward, of Ohio, and, in special manner, Ellis Ames, Esq., of Canton, a native of Bridgewater, whose accuracy and learning as an antiquary are in keeping with the readiness with which he imparts to others the results of his own labors.

And let us not forget the labors of him who was so eminently the *historian* of Bridgewater. Bound by the strong ties of kindred and affection to this his native town, he gave to it the fruits of the taste and diligence of an antiquary, in a volume which must ever serve as the storehouse of its early and genealogical annals.

Descended from one of the "forefathers," * and cherishing, as he did, a veneration for their memories, and the filial attachment of a son to Bridgewater, how would his gentle and genial spirit have rejoiced in this day! and with what delight would he have greeted these descendants of his early friends and associates; and of those, scarcely less his familiars, who felled the first forest-tree and planted the first cornfield on the spot where we are assembled!

Through a long and honored life, he shared alike the confidence of the public and the personal regard of his friends.

As an antiquary, he exhibited the unobtrusive and patient industry of "Old Mortality," in chipping out the fading memorials of a departed race.

And if, on this occasion, we bring forth, like the Romans of old, the images of the departed whose names we ought to recall, we should be doing injustice to ourselves, if, among them, we failed to give an honored place to that of *Mitchell*.

---

* *Experience Mitchell*, who came over in the "Anne," in 1623, the third ship that arrived.

In turning more directly to incidents of local history, it is obvious that time will admit of but little detail. All I can hope to do is to seize upon enough of these to serve as exponents of the moral, social, or political condition of its people from one period to another.

There is one conviction that presses upon the mind, in glancing along the pages of the early records of a state or town; and that is, how inadequately the actors in passing events measure their relative importance at the time of their occurrence. Time only furnishes the true test for this, when their relation to the after-events in history have been developed. If, for instance, we look into the records of the Provincial Congress, then in session, for any notice of the battle of Bunker Hill, though fought almost within hearing of its members, we find it incidentally spoken of as "the late attack of the king's troops at Bunker Hill;" little dreaming it was to be, in its consequence, one of the great events of the century. And so, on a smaller sphere, we look in vain, in the records of this town, for any thing more than a passing notice of what we now know were incidents of great historic interest.

While the location and allotments of their lands, the boundaries of their roads, and even the marks of ownership of their domestic animals, are carefully registered, Philip's war, the subversion of their charter, the usurpation of Andros, and the blotting-out of the political existence of one colony by the overshadowing growth of another, scarcely occupy a paragraph in these records.

There is enough to show that these were indeed exciting topics in the minds of the people of that day; but they left no declaration upon their records of the impression which these events had made.

The first recorded meeting of the inhabitants of the town was held on the 3d November, 1656.

Although one of the primary objects of these town organizations was to maintain a competent and pious ministry, I do not find any action upon the subject till January, 1660, when provision was made for the " carrying along the Lord's-Day exercise," by an offer of thirty pounds, or " twenty pounds and his diet," to Mr. Bunker, " to come hither, and supply our wants in the way of the ministry." This was indeed a day of small things. Money they had almost none; and even the corn which they made, to a considerable extent, a circulating medium, could only be produced by much toil, and often at the peril of life from a lurking foe.

Of their first meeting-house we know little. Such as it was, it served its purpose for a few years. But, in 1671, arrangements were made for the erection of one forty feet in length, twenty-six in width, and " fourteen feet studs," at an expense of " fourscore pounds," not including " the making of galleries or sealing." The means, however, for constructing this humble edifice were not raised by vote till 1673, when it was to be levied " ten pounds in money, ten pounds in Indian corn, and the rest in *marchandable* boards, at four shillings a *hundredth.*"

In the selection of a minister, the town seems to have been particularly fortunate. The records detail their agreement, in 1664, with " James Keith, a student of divinity," whereby, among other things, they were to cover the minister's house a second time; " to glaze the windows as soon as they could, provided they can get glass for boards;" and there were to be *two hundred bricks* furnished for constructing the chimneys, backs, hearths, and oven, payable in corn.

You may regard these as trifling details; but they tell, more vividly than any language can describe, the humble style in which these settlers lived, and the straits and circumstances to which they submitted, for so many years after they had taken upon themselves the character and duties of an independent municipality. Even their minister's house was to be glazed, and furnished with a brick chimney and oven, only on condition that they could procure the materials in exchange for the products of their own labor. Mr. Keith was a native of Scotland, had been educated at the university of Aberdeen, and was recommended to the people of Bridgewater by that renowned divine, Dr. Increase Mather. And, although the limits of these remarks will not allow me to speak of individual character in detail, it is pleasant to record that the connection of Mr. Keith with the people of his charge was alike honorable and creditable to both; and he seems to have stamped his own character upon this community. He preached his first sermon, it is said, from a rock in the open air, — typical of that rock on which his church should rest. He lived to see a population large enough for three parishes, and a minister settled over one of them besides his own,* and a considerable portion of another township carved from this; and was gathered to the reward of his labors, at the ripe age of seventy-six, in the year 1719.

It is sad to be reminded, as we glance over the pages of these records, how early the second generation began to illustrate, in practice, the truth of some of those rugged dogmas in theology which the first generation so stoutly maintained. There was, we have reason to fear, a spirit of depravity in the very earliest offshoots from the Pilgrim stock, when we read how, in 1686, the town chose " men to look after the boys on the sabbath days, that they be not disorderly; " and three grave gentlemen, — John Ames, senior, Thomas Snell, and Edward Mitchell, — worthy ancestors of a numerous and honored posterity, were selected for this difficult and responsible duty.

But without stopping to discuss points in polemical divinity, or why boys at that day required looking

---

* The South Parish was incorporated in 1716, and the Rev. Benjamin Allen ordained as the first pastor, July 9, 1718.

after, and leaving to modern reformers the graver question, why the tables have been so completely turned, that it is the boys now that look after the men, in their haste to discard the reverence as well as the theology of their fathers, I turn with more pleasure to the interest which, from an early period, the town has taken in the cause of education.

To Massachusetts is the honor due of having first devised free schools, in 1647, that "learning," in the beautiful language of the day, "might not be buried in the graves of their ancestors." In 1663, the court at Plymouth recommended a measure like this to the several towns.

But though, in the very infancy of the town, its inhabitants had shown the interest they felt in the cause of education, by contributing twelve pounds, in Indian corn, for the benefit of Harvard College, — for which, in behalf of that university, I now tender acknowledgments to their memory, — I do not find any corporate action for establishing schools within the town till about the year 1700, when "a scholar who came out from England, whose name is Thomas Martin," was engaged for four years to keep a school in four places in the town in each year, — three months in each place. And it was yet five years before they seem to have discovered, and even then but partially, what everybody now understands so well, — the superior qualifications of woman for instructing the young. They then voted "to provide four school-dames for to instruct small children in reading."

But, though entering late into the field, we are warranted, from its whole history, in believing that few towns have been more uniform or consistent in supplying to the young the means of education.* Though there were among the early settlers few who laid claim to much scholarship, there were none who wanted that general intelligence and practical good sense so much more useful to men in their condition. There was, in this respect, a remarkable uniformity among them, and scarcely, if any, less remarkable identity in their religious faith and observance of their moral duties. And, as an evidence of this, it is believed by those who have made it a subject of investigation, that drunkenness and its kindred vices were unknown among them; and not a single conviction of an inhabitant of the town, for any crime involving moral turpitude, was had while Plymouth existed as a colony.

When a better system of religion or of practical

---

* Since preparing this address, I have been kindly furnished, by a worthy and distinguished member of the Edson family, Rev. Dr. Edson, of Lowell, with extracts from two deeds, bearing date June 20, 1722, from Josiah Edson, known as "Justice Edson," son of Deacon Edson, named in the address. In one of these, he gives to the town of Bridgewater three parcels of land, "for the encouragement of a grammar school among them for ever;" and, in the other, he gives to the inhabitants of the South Precinct a tract of land, "for the promoting and encouraging of learning among them, . . . towards defraying the charge of a school or schools in said precinct."

These lands were the foundation of the "Edson Fund," which, upon the division of the town, was distributed among its several parts.

faith than this can be discovered, the world may begin to dispense with the old-fashioned notions of Robinson and Brewster. And yet it was not because the men of that day were wanting in spirit or energy or enterprise. We find among them, not only those who were competent to guide in the affairs of the town, but leading spirits in the colony, — Hayward, a military leader, when to be such was evidence of courage and capacity and of public confidence and respect, as well as a magistrate and a judge; the Bretts,* honored in church and state; Willis,† the first representative in the colonial General Court; the Edsons ‡ and the Mitchells. These are but among the names upon which the memory rests, when it dwells upon the early history of this spot.

But, invidious as it might seem to discriminate between these names, it would be far more so, if, in speaking of those who gave a character to the first generation, and whose teaching and influence trained up those who were to be worthy to succeed them, I passed over the wives and mothers who came here into the wilderness to give to the spot

---

* William Brett was ordained ruling elder of the church soon after Mr. Keith. Two of his sons were deacons of the church; and another, Elihu, a magistrate and justice of the C. C. Pleas.

† John Willis was first deacon of Rev. Mr. Keith's church, and represented the town in the Plymouth General Court for twenty-five years.

‡ Deacon Samuel Edson came from Salem, and settled in West Bridgewater. The name was among the most distinguished of the early families in the town. Col. Josiah was graduated at Cambridge in 1730, and was one of the mandamus counsellors at the commencement of the Revolution.

its strongest attraction, — the simple charm of home. They came here while the howl of the wolf was yet heard, from the deep forest around them, at midnight. Often and again did they clasp their little ones, with more than a mother's tenderness, as they saw the shadowy form of the savage stealthily prowling around their scattered dwellings; or waited in fearful suspense for the return of a husband from those bold forrays in which they sought for the foe in his lair.

But history does not tell of a mother's courage that quailed, or a woman's fortitude that shrunk, amidst these dangers.

It was the lessons and trainings of such mothers that supplied the nerve which carried the colonies through the Indian and French wars, and found every man a soldier, and in arms, as the alarm-cry went out over hill and through valley on the 19th April, 1775.

In considering the elements of growth and prosperity of the town, I ought not to pass over in silence the early development of the mechanical enterprise and skill which have so long distinguished its inhabitants. Though essentially an agricultural community, the useful and practical arts seem early to have found here a favorable soil.

There is something in the exhibition of the mechanic arts so nearly akin to the exercise of creative power, that we can never witness it without interest. But how ought this interest to be enhanced, when we are told, as we are by the venerable historian of the town, that it was here the first small-arms ever made in America were manufactured, the first solid cannon cast and bored, and the first thread of cotton spun by machinery; and that the first nail ever completely cut and headed by machinery, at a single operation, in the world, was made here! *

Who will estimate the debt that the world owes to the ingenuity of Orr † and his associates, and the inventive genius of Rogers, followed up, as they have been, by the enterprise and skill of the dwellers amidst these rural scenes? It has earned independent competency for the citizen; it has added countless value to the nation's wealth; and, though the period of which I am speaking was but the dawning of that day which made New England a mechanical and manufacturing as well as a commercial people, it supplied one of the strongest elements of our national union, when it made one part of this great continent dependent upon another for the sources of its wealth and prosperity, as well as of individual comfort and luxury.

---

* The first nails of this kind were manufactured by Samuel Rogers, of East Bridgewater.

† Hon. Hugh Orr, who was a member of the Senate in 1786, first manufactured small-arms and cannon here. He employed two brothers Barr to construct carding, spinning, and roping machines at his works in East Bridgewater, prior to 1786; and about that time, Thomas Somers, under direction of Mr. Orr, constructed other machines for carding, roping, and spinning cotton. About the same time, he employed one McClure to weave jeans and corduroys by hand, with a fly-shuttle. "About 1748, he made five thousand stands of arms for the Province of Massachusetts Bay, which were deposited in Castle William: nearly all, however, were carried off by the British when they evacuated the town of Boston."

But I am reluctantly compelled to forego any further detail of the incidents in the early history of the town.

The opening of the second century of her history found the colonies embroiled in the last of the " old French wars ; ". which was soon followed by the Sugar and Stamp Acts, and that course of measures which resulted in the war of the Revolution and the independence of our country.

But the century through whose vicissitudes she had passed had been working mighty changes in her condition.

The last of the " forefathers " and the "first-comers " had gone to their rest. The humble dwelling which Deacon Edson had reared here in 1646 had gathered around it near six hundred others, although the territory had been shorn of its proportions by the incorporation of Abington and Pembroke. The clack of the little mill which he had erected on "Town River," and which had fed these pioneers, had long been silent. The feeble church, which, under the guidance of Mr. Keith and Elder Brett, we had left struggling into life, had multiplied into five parishes, with their respective churches and pastors ; * while a population

---

* The South Parish was incorporated in 1716; and, at the time spoken of, Rev. John Shaw was its pastor. The East was incorporated in 1723; and Rev. John Angier was its pastor. The North was incorporated in 1738; and the Rev. John Porter its pastor. Titicut Parish was incorporated in 1743; and the Rev. Solomon Reed its pastor; while the Rev. Daniel Perkins, the successor of Mr. Keith, was the pastor of the original parish.

of near four thousand souls were scattered over this territory. Instead of sending, as she had done, for " a scholar that came out of England" to teach her schools, eleven of her own sons had themselves become scholars, and shared in the honors of our university.

All this, let us remember, had been the fruits, not of royal bounty, or even the distinguished advantages of superior local position. Her sons had brought with them no hoarded wealth, nor had any tide of successful foreign commerce enriched their coffers. They had gone through the struggles incident to the infancy, weakness, and poverty of such a settlement, had subdued a rugged soil, and had laid the foundations of a free and prosperous community too deep to be easily shaken.

And though this was followed by the long, wasting war of the Revolution, in which her resources were exhausted and her treasury bankrupt, there was within her a recuperative power which no difficulty could overcome, no adversity paralyze. She had within her a body of enterprising and intelligent men, — Pilgrims no longer, Puritans modified by the very world's respect which they had been winning, — who, severed for ever from the burdens and restraints of a foreign government, were now at liberty to give free play to the spirit that had descended upon them from the men of the " Mayflower."

But, before we venture to trace the effects of these

causes in their results, I should be doing injustice to the men who took part in the events of the opening scenes of the second century of the history of this community, if I omitted to speak of these a little more in detail. I have referred to the progress that had been then made from its condition a century earlier. But we ought not to be misled by such comparisons.

It would be pleasant if we could look in upon the social condition of the men of 1756, — their houses, their style of living, and the inventories of their goods and estates, — that we might compare them with 1856.

Neither time nor means within my command will admit of my doing this beyond the briefest notice. But a single fact may serve as an indication of what such a comparison might show.

In 1756, a tax was laid upon carriages in the Province, for the encouragement of the manufacture of linen. And it appears that there was neither coach nor chariot in all the Old Colony, and only four chaises, not one of which was in Bridgewater; and only four "chairs" were owned within the town.

But it should be remembered that the pillion and the horse-block had not yet disappeared before the march of modern refinement.

I have been furnished, through the kindness of the Register of Deeds in this county,* — for from every

---

* William S. Russell, Esq.

man, who ever had his home in Bridgewater, I have been sure of sympathy and aid, — with four inventories of estates from the probate-office: one from Plymouth, and another from Bridgewater, of a hundred years ago; the other two from the latter town, of an earlier date, one of which was of the Rev. Mr. Keith, in 1719.

Though it would be taxing your indulgence too far to give these in detail, permit me to glance at them, that we may see, for a moment, how far the luxuries of our fathers fell short of the necessaries of our own day.

The total of Mr. Keith's property — for preaching and property do not seem to have run in the same channel any more in that day than in this — amounted to a hundred and sixty-seven pounds eleven shillings, thirty pounds of which was his library, and seventy-two pounds household furniture, including *one looking-glass;* which might lead one to infer that he found the reflections on original sin, free agency, and the decrees which these ponderous tomes of polemical divinity suggested, far more suited to his taste than the reflection of his own benevolent countenance from the only mirror that his house afforded.

In the inventory of good Deacon Atwood, of Plymouth, in 1755, we cannot but be struck with an illustration of the proverbially superior thrift and foresight of the second over the first officer of every church.

Though possessed of more than ten times as much

estate as the venerable pastor of Bridgewater, he seems to have had a taste somewhat in contrast with that of the latter, and tending rather to looking-glasses than books; for we find he possessed three of the former, valued together at six pounds sixteen shillings and eightpence; while his whole library was appraised only at fourteen shillings and sixpence. And, while not a cent of silver-ware graced the cupboard of the pastor, the deacon was possessed of *five* large and *three* tea spoons of that precious metal.

This inventory, too, shows the change that had come over the spirit of the age, from the times of Carver and Standish, when every man was a soldier, or even that later period, when the church itself was turned into a fortress; for we find, as the only relics of his martial equipment, " one sword " and " one gun-lock."

But, instead of carnal weapons, we find him the possessor of one " negro man; " and that, while the good man's pew in his meeting-house was estimated at but twenty-three pounds six shillings and eightpence, this negro man, with the " negro bed " he occupied, were valued at forty-one pounds one shilling and fourpence.

Of the remaining inventory, that of Nathan Ames, of Bridgewater, in 1756, amounting to five hundred and twenty pounds, *five shillings* was the sum total of his library; while *one* looking-glass served the entire family, and one pillion was the only vehicle of transportation for the fairer members of it to church or to tea-parties.

In neither of these four inventories do we find either a watch or a clock. In neither of those of Bridgewater was there an article of silver-plate, even to a teaspoon. Nor was there, in either of the four, a carpet of any kind. And the nearest approach to a piano, in any of them, was the spinning-wheel, the hum of whose music was heard in every household in that day.

And yet we may judge, from a comparison of statistics, that her growth had been constant and healthy, and had more than kept pace with her sister towns.

In 1696, she stood, in the rate of taxation, the forty-eighth in the Province; in 1721, she had grown to be the sixteenth in valuation; in 1755, she stood the ninth in the Province, and above any other town in Plymouth County; and, in 1775, had risen to be the eighth in valuation in the whole Province of Massachusetts Bay.

And if we look, for a moment, at the part she took in the war of the Revolution, we shall find that she never withheld the fruits of her prosperity from the common cause in which they were engaged.

Let us bear in mind, that at no time during the war did her male population, above the age of sixteen, and able to bear arms, probably exceed a thousand.

I am unable even to approximate the number of her troops which were in the service under the call of the Province and State; but I have been shown seven requisitions for the Continental service, made upon the town from 1779 to 1781, which amounted to four hundred and twelve men in this space of three years.

When we remember what a large proportion of the productive labor of the town was thus withdrawn, we shall the more readily appreciate the extent of the burden which fell upon those who remained at home.

Making allowance for the depreciation of money, they must have paid, in 1776 and 1777, more than three thousand dollars in money.

In 1778 and 1779, they contributed each year, in shoes, stockings, and shirts, for the army, a number next to Boston itself; and the beef which they furnished upon requisition for the army, during 1780, must have amounted to more than five thousand dollars, at the rated value which it bore in the market.

I have mentioned these, not as showing the aggregate of her sacrifices, but as samples of what this town, in common with the whole of Massachusetts, contributed towards achieving the independence of our country.

I would gladly turn to the rolls of the Provincial and Continental troops of that period, and point out the names standing there; or go to the files of our treasury-office, and there sum up the amounts of money which were paid into the public chest by the people of this town to carry on that war.

But time will not admit of this; nor, if it did, would it do justice to the individual actors by whom it was contributed.

It is little more than an abstraction to tell how many men or how much money this or that town furnished during the Revolution.

We must go on to the farms and into the dwellings of the people of these towns to understand who were these men, and whence came this money. Mothers giving up their sons to the dangers of the field, and the still more fearful perils of the camp; husbands leaving to their wives the double task of the farm and the household, — are but among the incidents of these local histories. There is not a dwelling-house in any of these ancient towns, which was standing when that struggle began, that could not tell of days and nights of incessant toil, of self-denial, and patient, unrepining self-sacrifice on the part of its inmates, as, year after year, new burdens were imposed upon their feeble, wasting resources.

But I cannot dwell upon this point of our subject any farther than to say, that posterity will never know as they ought that the war of the Revolution was quite as essentially fought, and victory achieved, through what was done within these humble dwellings by the wives and mothers of that race, as by the prowess of arms and the courage of the battlefield.

From scenes like these, I turn to the changes which the century that was then opening has wrought within this community.

We sometimes forget how brief is the period within which, in our own country, great revolutions are effected. We measure the periods of early English history by centuries and by ages, — the six hundred years of the Roman dominion, the four hundred of Saxon rule, and the long succession of cycles and years before the human mind began to expand and grow free in the dawning light of civilization.

But here there are those still living in our own Commonwealth, within the space of whose life is embraced one-half of the entire period of this people's history.

And yet what changes do its social and economical statistics present!

The goodly territory for which, as its original title-deed shows, there were paid *seven coats, nine hatchets, eight hoes, twenty knives, four moose-skins, and ten and one-half yards of cotton*, has been multiplied into four thriving, independent communities. Its sons have gone out to people other regions, and swell the numbers of other communities; while its population has grown to more than three times the number which it contained when the century began. Wealth has been gathering here in a still greater ratio, till its aggregate has almost reached the sum of five millions of dollars. Her schools have multiplied, till fifty-three are open for the education of her twenty-three hundred children, besides three academies for the higher branches of instruction, and a normal school to give completeness to the system.

And if, in addition to these, we seek to measure the results of her manufacturing and mechanical industry, the statistics just published by the Legislature exhibit an aggregate of more than two million of dollars by the year.

There may be richer communities, there may be regions where Nature has been more lavish in her beauties and her bounty, there may be localities better known to fame, than that where we are now assembled; but where need we look for more certain elements of social and individual comfort and independence and happiness than are shared upon this portion of the heritage of a free people?

If, compared with some regions of ripe fertility, its soil be hardy, it breeds no miasma to paralyze or poison the arm that tills it.

If the breeze that sweeps over it be at times piercing and chill, it brings no pestilence in its train to blanch the ruddy glow of health. And if, under circumstances like these, the world has high claims upon those who have shared in the benefits and advantages which are here enjoyed, I greatly misjudge, or we should find, if we were to pursue the inquiry, that they have not been unfaithful to the trust with which they have been charged.

Delicacy forbids me to speak of the living by name, however glad we might be to honor the men who have shared the public confidence and our own. Of its citizens, five have represented this district in the Congress of the United States.* Another of her sons, after twenty-four years' service in the halls of Congress, closed his public career as the second officer of the Commonwealth, and has come back to finish a long and useful life amidst the scenes where that life began.†

And there have been others to whom it would be grateful to allude, who have stood before the public as the honored exponents, in church and commonwealth, of the tone of morals, and measure of intelligence, which have characterized this community.

But, while I have spoken of the local incidents and events, I have not attempted to follow into other communities, and upon wider or more distant spheres of action, the many who have gone out from the bosom of such a mother.

---

* Rev. Dr. Reed, Hon. Nahum Mitchell, Hon. William Baylies, Hon. Aaron Hobart, and Hon. Artemas Hale, the three last of whom were present on this occasion.

† Hon. John Reed, for many years of Yarmouth, which district he represented in Congress.

But go where you may, — into the country, or the populous marts of commerce; to the east or the west; through peopled regions of the old States, or the forest-homes and cities and villages of the new, — we find her sons, or her sons' sons, doing battle by the side of the hardy, the wise, and the strong men of the land. I find them healing the sick, preaching in the pulpit, and pleading at the bar, — on the bench, and in the halls of legislation. I see them reaping the fruits of industry and skill on the farm and in the workshop, and sharing the rewards of commercial enterprise and prosperous industry in a thousand forms.

I follow them also into the fields of literature, read the deep thoughts and treasured lore of the scholar, and feel my blood tingle and my soul refreshed by the inspired pages of the poet.

Do you ask for names with which to fill this picture, and with which to justify the language in which I have indulged? It was the son of a Bridgewater father,* who, when the fate of the British treaty hung in doubtful poise, and the cloud of war rose dark over an impoverished nation, in tones of eloquence that have never been surpassed, rolled back that cloud, and gave to his country peace and prosperity,

---

* Hon. Fisher Ames was the son of Dr. Nathaniel Ames, who removed from Bridgewater to Dedham, and a lineal descendant from one of the early settlers of the town.

that made her great among the greatest nations of the earth.

And, if time permitted me to speak of the men of my own profession here, the name of OAKES ANGIER would stand out prominently among the number by the acknowledged eminence he attained at the bar of the old colony.*

Take up the catalogue of those who, on the bench and in the councils of the State and nation, have held places of honor and trust, and count up how many of the names that you find there you have read in those records, and upon the mossy headstones which tell where your own kindred are sleeping, — the Shaws, the Haywards, the Whitmans, the Mitchells, the Reeds, the Ameses, the Forbeses, and the Sangers.†

---

* The following extract, from an epitaph which is inscribed upon a monument in the ancient cemetery in West Bridgewater, is from the pen of the late Hon. Judge Davis: —

"OAKES ANGIER, Esq., BARRISTER-AT-LAW, departed this life, Sept. 1, 1786, in the forty-first year of his age, and here lies interred.

"With a mind vigorous and penetrating, assiduous and indefatigable in business, he soon arrived to eminence in his profession.

"Seventeen years' practice at the bar, with fidelity, integrity, and ability, established his reputation and improved his fortune, but too fatally injured his constitution in the meridian of life."

Judge Davis, Lieutenant-Governor Robbins, and the late Hon. Pliny Merrick, father of Judge Merrick, of the Supreme Judicial Court, were among those who studied law in his office.

† Without undertaking to enumerate these, it may be proper to name Chief Justice Shaw, grandson of the Rev. John Shaw; Hon. Ezekiel Whitman, late Chief Justice of Maine; Hon. Charles E. Forbes, late Judge of our Supreme Court; and Hon. George P. Sanger, Judge of the Court of Common Pleas, the grandson of Rev. Dr. Sanger.

And as I glance at the roll of the present Congress, and find a name there three times repeated, I shall hardly be charged with indelicacy if I recall the part which the first who bore it took, after his traditionary connection with the Massachusetts colony had ceased, as one of the Duxbury men, in the event which we are now commemorating.*

Or, if we look for what her sons have done in the fields of literature, though time forbids me to dwell upon so pleasant a theme, — while we have no cause to fear that poesy will not be found this day wedded to a name now familiar here, — if I speak of the past, I have only to open upon that sublime triumph of genius over death itself, the "Thanatopsis," to know that one at least of the "Poets of America" has but added renown to a name which is associated with the memory of the dwellers upon this spot.†

I have spoken of the past; but what am I to say of the future of this people, and of our common coun-

---

* John Washburn is believed to have been the first Secretary of the Massachusetts Company before the transfer of the charter to Massachusetts. He was born in Evesham, in the county of Worcester, and settled in Duxbury as early as 1632, where he was joined by his family, consisting of his wife and two sons, in 1635. His son John married a daughter of Experience Mitchell; and from him the branches now so numerous and widely scattered have descended. One of his sons married a grand-daughter of Mary Chilton, from whom have sprung a numerous posterity, and through which the writer is allowed to lay claim to affinity with one of the early settlers of this town.

† Bryant — for he needs no other distinctive name — was the son of a physician born in Bridgewater, himself the son of a physician who was born and always resided in this town.

try? There are those to whose vision a darker cloud is rising over the land than has ever threatened it before, — a cloud of discord and disunion, from which even the reflected glory of the past gives back no bow of hope.

And it cannot be denied that there is enough to excite deep apprehension in the stoutest heart in the events of the last few weeks.

We look in vain for protection or redress in the excited passions of political strife. The only hope that seems left to us is to be just to ourselves; to keep this moral malaria within its own sphere, by shutting out its influence from our borders. Let there be union of heart and union of sentiment among free men; let the *united* action of one section no longer triumph in the divisions and personal and party jealousies of the other, — and the hour of danger and apprehension will have passed.

And is there not hope from the very extremity of danger that we seem to have reached? Will not the blood that has been spilt in the senate-chamber of the nation — in a brutal and cowardly blow, struck, through a representative of a free State, at constitutional right, the honor of our own honored Commonwealth, and the cause of liberty in the world — become an element to cement the divided counsels and call forth the united action of every man who dares or deserves to be free? Let this be done, and every thing is done; every other element is already shaped at our hand.

From elements such as we have been considering, there can come no danger to the cause of human liberty and human progress. The little community of whose history I have so imperfectly spoken, is but one of a thousand others where there is a reserved power cherished and kept alive, and ready for any emergency.

Neither schools nor churches, nor the hallowed associations of home, have ceased to educate and refine the intellect and affections; nor have free discussion and a free press become impotent to arouse to action a love of country among a people to whom the past has so much of pride, and the future is so full of promise.

Fraud may triumph for a day, and injustice may wreak its power here and there upon its victim; but, thank God, there is a power greater than these, — a power that breaks through the chains of error, and will bid man at last be free.

> "Truth, crushed to earth, will rise again;
> The eternal years of God are hers."

A mighty destiny is before us as a people. The glorious problem of human development and human freedom is being wrought out on the theatre of this vast republic. In its accomplishment will be seen the fruits of that enterprise which was cradled in that little church at Scrooby, and reared by the watchfulness and prayers of good men, and found a congenial home here two hundred and thirty-six years ago.

Every spot in the old colony is rich with the deeds and virtues of the Puritans and their descendants. Every spot has sent forth seed, which, borne like that of the thistle on every wind, has been scattered and has sprung up in every region of this continent.

Reversing the law that seeks to renovate the decrepitude of years by transfusing young blood into the torpid veins of age, the blood that has gone out from these ancient bodies politic is found invigorating and infusing fresh life into the young communities that have sprung up in the forests of the East and along the rivers and prairies of the constantly widening West.

Wherever white men have fixed their homes, among them have these sons of the old colony been busy in rearing the schoolhouse and the church, in scattering New-England notions and sentiments, and planting institutions which have tempered and modified and assimilated the masses that have been crowding to our shores, into a national, free, American republic. They forget the moral power of that engine and these influences who look with such seeming apprehension upon the influx of strangers from the Old World; as if the mere physical strength of thews and sinews could stand against the moral and intellectual power of the trained, educated, self-governed denizens of the soil!

In this great work of harmonizing and nationalizing our common country; in carrying, as it were, the borders of New England clear across this wide continent; in planting new Plymouths on the shores of the Pacific, and new Bridgewaters in the valleys of the West, — old Bridgewater has borne an honored part.

And now her sons and her sons' sons have come together, around the old domestic hearthstone, to renew, in the memories and associations of the past, the ties that once bound them to this spot, and the obligations they owe to their country and their generation to spread and perpetuate the good old sentiments and habits and opinions that found so congenial a soil in this early home of our fathers.

And, if they find that prosperous industry and thrift have been at work in changing old familiar scenes, the generous heart that bade even the stranger welcome in days of yore still beats as warmly as it then did; and, though the latch-string has disappeared in the progress of refinement, hospitality still opens its door as wide to all who would come and share its comforts and its courtesies.

Two centuries have now closed their record of the fortunes of this people, and left their memorial in the brief yet crowded page of their history.

We can go back, at a glance, to the feeble, struggling infancy and childhood of this community; but its future we can only read in the light of the past. In that light we have every thing to hope, and little to apprehend.

A new century is opening amidst the stirring scenes, the energized thought, the free, onward movement, of the nineteenth century, developed in its full maturity.

It will close over other actors, and after changes which no human vision can now reach; and happy will it be if it shall witness fruition as unimpaired and hopes as bright as those which mark its opening day.

And standing, as we do, on that narrow point, where, turning from the past, fancy calls up the shadowy forms that crowd the vision of the future, I cannot better close this poor effort to do justice to our theme than in the language of one whom any community might be proud to call her own: —

> "My heart is awed within me when I think
> Of the great miracle that still goes on
> In silence round me, — the perpetual work
> Of a creation finished, yet renewed
> For ever.
>   Lo! all grow old, and die; but see again,
> How, on the faltering footsteps of decay,
> Youth presses!
>   Life mocks the idle hate
> Of his arch-enemy Death; yea, seats himself
> Upon the tyrant's throne, — the sepulchre, —
> And of the triumphs of his ghastly foe
> Makes his own nourishment."

The Boston Brass Band played an appropriate piece of music.

JAMES REED, A. B., of Boston, delivered the following —

POEM.

TIME has always been a river,
    And eternity its sea,
Where, upon some leaf or sliver,
    Men have floated ceaselessly.

Now 'midst verdure never ending,
    Now 'mid deserts brown and bare,
Is the mighty river wending,
    Who can tell us whence or where?

Ever changing is the current
    Of the vast, mysterious stream :
Here it swells into a torrent,
    There 'tis like an infant's dream.

We, who down the stream are sailing,
    Guide our craft in different ways;
Some with mournful noise of wailing,
    Some with songs of hope and praise.

Down we float 'mid joy and sorrow,
    Hatred cold and friendship fond,
Craving sunshine for the morrow
    In the depths which lie beyond.

Why keep crying, "Whither? whither?
   Watchman, tell us of the night"?
Surely He who brought us hither
   Will direct our course aright.

As the river, circling ever,
   Once again will come in sight
Of its fountain, witnessed never
   Since it first embraced the light; —

So upon this golden morning,
   On the bosom of the waves,
For a timely word of warning,
   Come we to our fathers' graves.

Looking o'er the fields and meadows
   Which unnoticed lie between,
Indistinct as evening shadows,
   Figures of the past are seen.

As the sun is ever lifting
   Ocean's vapors to the sky,
So from out the past come drifting
   Memories of the days gone by.

Fathers, mothers, rise before us,
   Quick to hear affection's call;
While the arch which closes o'er us
   Shields the homesteads of us all.

Down we float, and leave to others
   Words of hate and angry scorn;
While we turn, a band of brothers,
   Back to the ancestral morn.

Down we float, and soon behind us
   Leave we present scenes and men,
Wondering where this day will find us,
   Rolled by centuries round again.

Down we float, believing, knowing,
　　That no evil can befall,
When, as from a sun, is flowing
　　Love unbounded for us all.

Never even can disaster
　　Cast its shadow o'er a dream,
If we let the perfect Master
　　Guide our passage down the stream.

———

There have been days, as well we know,
Before this present summer morn;
And, trusting those who tell us so,
Time was ere we ourselves were born.

And, looking down the rugged hill
Up which the past has borne the cross,
The landscape sleeps, serene and still,
Though overgrown with weeds and moss.

Full many an anxious heart has beat
With love for Jack or love for Jill;
Full many a pair of pretty feet
Has danced or loitered up the hill.

But what of that? In bygone things
We seldom claim to have a share;
Content with what the present brings,
If only what it brings be fair.

So scenes will often pass from mind
Which never should have been forgot;
Thus, not so long ago, we find
The town of Bridgewater was not.

The town of Bridgewater was not:
How comes it that the town has been?
'Twas purchased in a single lot
Of famous old Ousamequin.

Then fifty-four stout men arose
To take the land for good or worse,
Whose honest names will do for prose,
But never could be meant for verse.

How high must be the poet's claims
Who meets no mental scrapes and rubs
In putting into verse the names, —
Experience Mitchell, William Tubbs!

For though experience teaches well,
And tubs on their own bottoms stand,
Theirs hardly is the magic spell
By which a verse is made to hand.

Experience, if he married well,
To lively Sorrow linked his life;
Nor would it be so strange to tell
If *hoops* encircled Tubbs's wife.

Experience, if a child he had,
To call her Wisdom scarce could fail;
While Tubbs need not have felt so bad
If his turned out a little *pale*.

Forgive, if aught which I have said,
Experience, seems to mar thy fame:
A blessing, Tubbs, upon thy head;
I jested only with thy name.

A blessing on the brave old men
From whom we claim a common birth;
Whom earth will not behold again,
Whose virtues cannot pass from earth.

All honor to their hoary hair!
They are not dead, — they gently sleep:
For us were all their grief and care;
They sowed the field which we shall reap.

Oh! chide not him who loves to roam
Among the relics of the past;
Who calls one little spot his home,
And clings around it to the last.

And though his lineage he may track
With something of an honest pride,
Who calls it crime to wander back
Among the noble who have died?

Not how our fathers passed their days
The present bard designs to sing;
Nor yet the wreath of feeble praise
Around their honored brows to fling: —

But from the volume of their woes
One simple chapter will he take,
Wherein old Winter sheds his snows;
But they live on for Freedom's sake.

Next come the joys which all must feel
When past are Winter's dreary hours;
When life from death begins to steal,
And rosy Spring brings back the flowers.

How fearful the tempests which howl through the winters,
  Pursuing the mariner over the sea;
Which dash the stout heart of the oak into splinters,
  And show us how terrible Nature can be!

We quietly sit by the family-fire,
  And heed not the tempest which howls at the door,
But pile up the logs ever higher and higher,
  Defying old Winter a thousand times o'er.

"Come in if thou canst, and give over thy moaning,
  Who turnest to ice what thou breathest upon,
And tell us how many this moment are groaning
  O'er mischief which thou in thy madness hast done; —

"How many are wrapping their garments around them,
　　Resigning themselves to thy rage in despair;
How many lie dead where by chance thou hast found them,
　　Who had not a moment to murmur a prayer.

"Good luck betide those who are hopefully braving,
　　Thou cruel old monster, the strength of thine ire, —
The heart-broken wretches who fain would be saving
　　Their one spark of life by their one spark of fire!"

Oh, pity! Why need we an instant to borrow
　　A counterfeit sadness from poem or tale,
When more than our hearts can imagine of sorrow
　　Goes moaning about on the wings of the gale?

We gather to-day beneath Summer's green arches,
　　And Winter's dominion appears like a dream;
But steadily onward old Time ever marches,
　　And soon the bright Summer a vision will seem.

We look o'er a country where Plenty is reigning,
　　And pouring the blessings of Peace from her horn,
And little imagine the good we are gaining
　　From those who had died ere our fathers were born.

They came o'er the sea on a journey of peril;
　　Like mists of the morning were scattered their foes;
And fat grew the land which before had been sterile,
　　And straightway the wilderness bloomed like the rose.

With logs for their dwellings, and bears for their neighbors,
　　And men in the forest more fearful than bears,
What heart could prefigure the end of their labors,
　　Or half of the glory and praise which are theirs?

And, oh! when the tempests of winter were howling,
　　And claiming admittance through cranny and crack;
When every thing deadly around them was prowling,
　　And heaven's blue arches were curtained with black; —

When out of the woods came the yell of the foeman,
    The heart-broken accent of maddened despair,
And swiftly the shaft of the bloody-red bowman
    Flew, piercing the snow-flakes which stifled the air, —

How strangely contrasted the sounds which were blending —
    The din of the storm, and the foeman's wild cries —
With prayers which were evermore gently ascending
    To Him who shall wipe away tears from all eyes!

And fondly sped backward their thoughts o'er the waters,
    To homes which were happy, and might be their own, —
Where England keeps watch o'er her sons and her daughters,
    But treats not so kindly the birds which have flown.

A truce to old Winter: though dreadful the curses
    Which follow, like birds of the night, in his train,
We love him almost for the child which he nurses, —
    Our beautiful Spring, with her sunlight and rain.

Who closes the door when the blithe little maiden
    Comes tripping along with her basket of flowers?
Who loves not the treasures with which she is laden,
    Whose smile is the sunshine, whose tears are the showers?

The hearts of our fathers she filled with her gladness
    When o'er them her sweet-laden breezes she poured,
In place of the clouds with their shadows of sadness,
    Which seemed like the menacing wrath of the Lord.

No more need the men their alarms to dissemble,
    The women to cover their faces for fright;
No more need the children to listen and tremble,
    Like lambs at the tread of the wolf, over night.

The clouds were not all from the firmament driven,
    When Winter had taken his leave of the stage;
But Spring set her rainbow of hope in the heaven, —
    The spirit of childhood for that of old age.

What load is so great that it cannot be lightened,
　　What heart is so old that it will not grow young,
What future so dark that it will not be brightened,
　　If brooks have but murmured, and birds have but sung?

When sunny-faced Spring, through a million of voices,
　　Proclaims to the earth that her advent is near,
The kindly old mother as truly rejoices
　　As when the first sunlight awoke the first year.

From Winter's deep slumbers she joyfully rises,
　　And flings a green mantle o'er valleys and hills;
Then decks herself out in the gems which she prizes, —
　　A necklace of lakes, and a girdle of rills.

　　This day, two centuries ago,
　　Beneath this sky, our fathers came,
　　Resolved to plant, for weal or woe,
　　The scions of an honest name.

　　To-day, two centuries have fled;
　　And we, their children, come to see
　　If what they planted here is dead,
　　Or fruit is hanging from the tree.

　　As o'er recorded time we look,
　　And then into the present glare,
　　We wonder, as we close the book,
　　Which picture we must judge more fair.

　　Is that which hangs upon the bough
　　The glory of the parent stem?
　　Or were they wiser then than now?
　　And borrow we our light from them?

　　No matter. This at least we know,
　　That, whether bright or dim our fires,
　　They must with wondrous lustre glow
　　To match the splendor of our sires.

Our lots have fallen in different times:
They lived in winter, cold and drear;
But we are listening to the chimes
With which the spring awakes the year.

Their path was strewn with stony cares,
But ours is full of hopeful flowers;
The labor and the pain were theirs,
While all the fruitful joy is ours.

How wondrous is the lapse of time,
The heart of man no more conceives
Than children of a southern clime
Can think of plants without their leaves.

Recall the days when wheels were rare,
And stages never passed the town;
When, pillion-back, a loving pair
Rode gravely jogging up and down.

What need of stage or omnibus,
Without a road where wheels could range?
Strange passing that would be for us;
In truth, it would be passing strange.

How wide their eyes would open now,
If they could see what we have done;
Could see the fruit upon the bough,
Which ripens in the morning sun!

How pleasant it would be to show
Our gallery of modern arts,
Where all the powers which move below
Are taught to play respective parts!

How full their souls would be of wonder,
And how our wiser selves would laugh,
If they beheld that son of thunder,
Which we have called the telegraph!

"My ancient friend," their sons might say,
"Observe our modes of locomotion:
Instead of fifty miles a day,
A week will nearly cross the ocean."

"I know, my son," the sage replies,
"The age of pillions long is past;
But now the danger in my eyes
Is lest you get a bit too fast."

"Again, good sires, be pleased to see
Another jewel in our crown:
The sun takes portraits, so that we
To future time can hand them down."

"My sons," 'tis answered with a frown,
"If you forget the shaving-cup,
Though you may hand your faces down,
We'll thank you not to hand them up."

What man who sees the ages rise,
And notes the changes which they bring,
Can marvel that our partial eyes
Should judge the present season spring?

From out the darkness of the past
So many wonders have been born,
That we appear to sit at last
Upon the threshold of the morn.

A wondrous stern and sturdy stock
Was that from which we claim descent:
Their faith was like the steadfast rock;
Their lives, a deathless monument.

No doubtful hate within them burning
Impelled them to a doubtful field;
But hearts resolved upon returning,
Like Spartan, with or on the shield.

Can wrong usurp the place of right?
And can the changeless laws be changed?
Or must the darkness and the light,
Divided once, be kept estranged?

In truth, what we esteem a sin
Was virtue in the days of old;
And what they spurned as glittering tin,
We treasure as the solid gold.

We like, the most of us, to dance,
Or spend an evening at a play;
While they would rather take their chance
At drinking poison any day.

They thought it was a gracious deed
To bring a Quaker to his end;
While only in extremest need
We kill a foe, much less a *friend*.

And how their pious eyes would glow
When witches at the stake were burned!
But we caress our witches so,
That all the tables now are turned.

Although a witch may be a thing
Which should be rapped upon the head,
'Tis time to stop our cudgelling,
If she will rap us back when dead.

With guilt which they trod in the dust,
Their sons, we hope, are gently dealing:
'Tis one thing to be strictly just,
Another to have kindly feeling.

But while forgiveness we bestow
Upon the sinner, not the sin,
We must not fail to strike the blow
When fear alone would hold us in.

A little more of self-respect,
While travelling in the path of right,
Would make our journey more direct,
And throw more day upon our night.

Though age may often find it hard
To gather all its dues from youth,
'Tis better than that blind regard
Should swallow up the living truth.

The honest lives our fathers led,
Blame ye who can defend your own:
"The sinless man," it has been said,
"Shall be the first to cast a stone."

Their virtues we must all applaud,
Who have a care for real worth:
If such were scattered more abroad,
'Twould be the better for the earth.

How oft from yonder spire have rung
The echoes of the sabbath-bell! —
A summons sweet to old and young
To draw the truth from truth's own well.

The word of God, from lips inspired,
They heard, and, hearing, they adored;
And, though the preacher they admired,
They came to worship but the Lord.

Within the mists of bygone days,
Which wrap the past as in a cloud,
Three reverend men are giving praise,
And asking blessings on the crowd.

A blessing in the name of truth
Upon the shepherds of the sheep,
Who labored from the dawn of youth,
Till evening brought the hour of sleep!

More faithful servants who can find
Than these to work the work of God?
What men have left more fruit behind
To mark the path in which they trod?

And thou, whose honored name is mine
To tarnish or to honor still,
For whom no human hand can twine
A wreath which will become thee ill, —

Be happy, in the name of those
Whom thou has taught the ways of right,
In realms where duty pleasure grows,
And where the blind receive their sight.

Now, the benediction uttered,
   Draws our service to its close:
Soon must parting words be muttered,
   Soon must evening bring repose.

Then our holiday is over,
   And we travel, every one, —
Father, mother, sister, lover, —
   Onward to the setting sun.

Loving, striving, wishing, hoping,
   Fond and anxious hearts we bear;
Sadly now through darkness groping,
   Bending now to breathe a prayer.

Soon the lover and the maiden
   Are the husband and the wife,
And, with common burdens laden,
   Sail adown the stream of life; —

Soon the father and the mother
   Teach the child the way of truth;
Soon the sister and the brother
   Ripen into blushing youth.

Then comes age, as sweet and simple
　　As the infant newly born, —
Placid lake without a dimple,
　　Waiting for the coming morn.

Waiting! Then the morn is coming,
　　Reddening all the eastern sky:
Now is heard a distant humming
　　From the day which will not die.

Waiting! All of us are waiting;
　　And the youngest child who hears,
Even now his bark is freighting
　　With its load of hopes and fears.

When the next assembly gathers
　　On the soil which now we tread,
We shall be the honored fathers,
　　Numbered with the living dead.

In the mail of self-denial
　　We must arm us for the fray,
Ere the hands upon the dial
　　Mark the limits of the day.

Honest lives, not empty phrases,
　　Are the stuff to make a name
Worthy of our children's praises,
　　Worthy of our fathers' fame.

Still before us lies the river,
　　With its tides of good and ill:
There we may lie mute, and shiver,
　　Or be sailing where we will.

Strike when iron hoofs are tramping
　　O'er the bodies of the just!
Strike when guilty Power is stamping
　　Wounded Freedom in the dust!

Strike when honest men are lying
  By the hands of cowards slain!
Strike when Abel's blood is crying
  Vengeance on the guilty Cain!

Love the slayer and the slaughtered!
  And, as love grows strong with years,
May their future graves be watered
  With our kind, forgiving tears!

The following Hymn, written by Rev. DANIEL HUNTINGTON, of New London, was sung by the assembly, to the tune of "Old Hundred:" —

GOD of our fathers! hear the song
Their grateful sons united raise,
While round their hallowed graves we throng
To think and speak of other days, —

Those days of toil and peril, when,
In faith and love that conquered fear,
They bought the fields of savage men,
And reared their homes and altars here.

To thee their daily vows were paid;
To thee their hearts and lives were given;
And, by thy guidance and thine aid,
They trod their pilgrim-path to heaven.

Rich is the heritage we claim,
Whom thou hast made their favored heirs, —
Their cherished faith, their honest fame,
Their love, their counsels, and their prayers.

> They left us freedom, honor, truth:
> Oh, may these rich bequests descend
> From sire to son, from age to youth,
> And bless our land till time shall end!
>
> So, as successive centuries roll,
> When we shall long have passed away,
> Here may our sons, with heart and soul,
> Still hail Bridgewater's natal day.

A Benediction was pronounced by Rev. BAALIS SANFORD, of East Bridgewater.

A recess of twenty minutes was taken, when a procession was formed, of persons holding tickets for the dinner, in the same order as the procession of the morning, and marched to the pavilion erected on the easterly side of the main street, between the houses of William Copeland and Jonas Leonard, where J. B. Smith, of Boston, had provided one of his excellent dinners for a thousand persons. A blessing was invoked by the venerable Dr. KENDALL, of Plymouth. After those who sat at the tables had partaken of the bountiful refreshments which had been laid before them, thanks were returned by Rev. Dr. EDSON, of Lowell.

Hon. JOHN A. SHAW, the President of the day, then delivered the following Address: —

FELLOW-CITIZENS AND DESCENDANTS OF THE GOOD OLD
TOWN OF BRIDGEWATER, —

The pleasant duty has been assigned me of bidding you welcome on this festal occasion. I gladly bid you a *hearty* welcome to this festive board, to the intellectual repast, and to all the hallowed associations of this auspicious day. It is a great, a joyous day, which brings together so many of us at the old family homestead, in this loveliest month of all the year, when Nature is putting on her beautiful garments, and decking herself in flowers.

Ladies, you are especially welcome; for it would be dark around our hearth-stone without the light of woman's smile. We hail your presence at this board as the companion and equal of man. Nothing truly good or great ever has been or can be effected without the aid of woman. She was the helpmate of our fathers: she cheered them in their toils and privations at the same time that she shared them.

Though many of us are now in each other's presence for the first time, we are not strangers to each other, but brothers and sisters of one and the same household. Yes, ladies and gentlemen, a common bond unites us as the members of one great family; for we all cherish in common a grateful remembrance of our pious ancestors, whose presence hallowed these regions two hundred years ago. We embalm alike in our hearts the recollection of their toils, their privations, and their dangers; of their stern integrity, and strict purity of life. We reverence alike their unfaltering trust in God; their indomitable perseverance; and their determined purpose to enjoy liberty of conscience, and transmit the same to posterity. While cherishing these precious reminiscences of our pious forefathers, we are not strangers to each other, but brethren of one heart and of one spirit.

In welcoming you, ladies and gentlemen, to a participation in this day's services, we cannot point you to any localities in our neighborhood which are renowned in the world's history. No great battle-fields, on which the fate of nations has been decided, are near us. We can direct your admiring gaze to no Bunker Hill, no Heights of Dorchester. But look around, and you will see the fields on which have been achieved the no less glorious triumphs of peace, — fields which, generations ago, were cleared of their primeval forest growth and cultivated by the hands of men of whom the Old World was not worthy; men of whom it was said, that "God sifted a whole nation to obtain precious seed for sowing this Western World." To such men, and their immediate successors, we can look back as our progenitors; and, when our eyes rest on these scenes of their labors, it is a grateful reflection that these territories were fairly purchased of their aboriginal possessors, and freely granted by them to our fathers. Not far from the place where we are now assembled, you can read the humble memorials of these men, where rest their mortal remains: —

> "Their name, their years, spelt by the unlettered Muse,
> The place of fame and elegy supply;
> And many a holy text around she strews,
> That teach the rustic moralist to die."

In setting apart this day for the commemoration of those good men who first settled the ancient town, we express our gratitude to our Father in heaven for having given us an ancestry to whom we can ever look back with reverence. The "Memoir of Plymouth Colony,"* when speaking of Bridgewater as it was in 1692, remarks, that "the foundation was laid for a population, which subsequently has been distinguished for correct moral habits, enterprise, industry, and learning." From another source † we have the following record, made a hundred and thirty-nine years ago, in these words: "The New-English Bridgewater has been a town favored of God. It was planted a noble vine. The first

---

* Francis Baylies. † Increase and Cotton Mather.

planters of it were a set of people who made religion their main interest, and it became their glory."

Although the names of our ancestors are not emblazoned on the rolls of fame, they gave the first direction and impulse to a community, which, from their days to the present time, has been steadily moving onward with the onward march of this noble Commonwealth, of this mighty nation. Though they were not themselves of those whom the world calls great, the example of their virtues, and the spirit they bequeathed to their posterity, have raised up not a few among their descendants, whose names will live on the page of history, and whose services will be felt and appreciated, long after their frail bodies shall have mouldered into dust. In confirmation of this, I will remind you of Fisher Ames, the enlightened and pure-hearted statesman, whose eloquent tongue uttered the accents of an angel with an angel's power.

Two gentlemen* are now living, descendants of Bridgewater, who have been the chief magistrates of this Commonwealth; one of whom, as you know, has done us the honor of being our orator to-day, and to whose eloquent words we have listened with deepest interest. Also there are now present at this board our venerable Chief Justice, and another venerable man, the late Chief Justice of the State of Maine, likewise descendants † of the ancient town. Of the five ex-members of Congress now residing within our borders, four of whom honor us with their presence to-day, two were born in the old town, one of whom has also recently been our Lieutenant-Governor.‡ Three members of the present Congress are among her descendants.§ And one of the beautiful odes which have moved our hearts to-day reminds us that there are those ‖ among her sons who can —

"Wake to ecstasy the living lyre."

---

* Marcus Morton and Emory Washburn.
† Lemuel Shaw and Ezekiel Whitman.
‡ John Reed.   § The Washburns.   ‖ W. C. Bryant.

Such was the prosperity of the ancient Bridgewater under the wise counsels of its early settlers, that it contained, one hundred years ago, a population of thirty-seven hundred; a greater number of inhabitants to the square mile, at that early day, than two-thirds of the States of this Union have at the present time, old Virginia being one of them. Our population is now approaching fourfold what it then was; for which increase we are principally indebted to North Bridgewater, which has at the present time as numerous a population as the whole of the old town had when it was divided in 1821. The population is now towards two hundred to the square mile; considerably greater than the average of our populous Commonwealth, the most compactly peopled State in the Union. Indeed, but few countries of Europe have as many inhabitants to the square mile as the territory about us; and this with no extraordinary natural advantages, but by only heeding the lessons of those who have gone before us, — men who bequeathed in their example the virtues of industry, frugality, and perseverance, the fear of God, and respect for the rights of man.

It is not in a boastful spirit that we speak of the prosperity which this day surrounds us, but, we trust, in the spirit of gratitude to that beneficent Being, from whose free bounty comes every thing which gladdens our sojourn upon earth, — every thing that gives us the hope of immortality beyond it. We should be the unworthy descendants of those good men of whom this day vividly reminds us, could we assemble in the midst of all that blesses life, and not be mindful of those religious hopes and aspirations which brought our Pilgrim Fathers across the broad Atlantic; which encouraged and cheered them on to encounter the perils and hardships of an unknown shore, a boundless wilderness, and a race of savage men, and without which we should be but little better than insects of a day.

Descendants of the ancient Bridgewater, and you who now inhabit her territory, we know from authentic records what the condition of the region round about was two hundred years ago. We also know that this district of country was prosperous and comparatively wealthy and populous one hundred years ago. Our eyes see and our hearts feel what it is to-day. But who can lift the veil which covers the future from our view? Who can look down the long vista to 1956, and describe to us the Bridgewaters of that day? Who can inform us respecting the men and women who will assemble on the 3d of June in that year to do honor to the memory of their ancestors?

Though the reality is wisely concealed from all but Him who sees the end from the beginning, we cannot doubt that a glorious destiny is in reserve for those who are to follow us. The history of the world declares the onward and upward course of man, notwithstanding he sometimes relapses. Auspicious omens cheer us on, though clouds sometimes darken the horizon. And, though wrong and outrage may triumph for a season, there is a Power which causes even "the wrath of man to praise him." Though we are not prophets, we are taught by those who were, that the human race was placed on earth for a far nobler state of society than the world has ever seen; that the religion of the Saviour will yet enlighten and elevate all nations. We know that his prayer must yet be answered, and God's "will be done on earth as it is in heaven."

What revolutions, what convulsions, what reverses, may precede the promised age, or when its full-orbed splendor shall illuminate the world, it is not ours to know. It is enough for us to be assured, that the Sun of Righteousness will, at some future day, shed his beams on every land, and that the love of God and man will be the controlling spirit of our race. And just so far as this spirit becomes the rule of action, just so far, and no farther, will earth become a paradise. For what is man without morals? What are morals without religious principle?

Let our countrymen but give heed to the declaration of

our political father, that "the preservation of our Union is of infinite moment both to our collective and individual happiness, and that we ought to frown indignantly upon every attempt to alienate one portion of our country from the rest;" let them believe with him, that "religion and morality are indispensable supports of all the dispositions and habits which lead to political prosperity;" let such instructions as these words of him, who was "first in the hearts of his countrymen," but guide the conduct of the people of these United States, — and the century on which we are entering to-day will witness a progress no less wonderful than the last, as regards both our nation, our State, and our neighborhood.

But I must forbear, and keep you back no longer from the intellectual repast which the eloquent men whom I see around me are prepared to set before you.

I have only to say again, Welcome, thrice welcome, ladies and gentlemen, to the hallowed associations and all the enjoyments of this Second Centennial Day of Bridgewater.

BENJAMIN W. HARRIS, Esq., the Toastmaster, then announced the regular sentiments as follows: —

1. "*The Two Hundredth Anniversary of the Incorporation of Bridgewater* — The children of the *ancient* town are assembled from the north and the south, the east and the west, to do *honor* to their parent; and may their days be *long* in the land, according to the promise!"

To this sentiment, Hon. EZEKIEL WHITMAN, of East Bridgewater, made the following remarks: —

MR. PRESIDENT, — I presume I am called upon, on the present occasion, on account of my being an octogenarian, and, therefore, as being able to carry my recollection back to a remote period.

I spent my youthful days, principally, till twenty-three years of age, in the good old town of Bridgewater; afterwards I resided in Maine till within a few years past; and I can say with the celebrated Goldsmith, that —

> "In all my wanderings through this world of care,
> In all my griefs, — and God has given my share, —
> I still had hopes, my latest hours to crown,
> Amidst these humble bowers to lay me down;
> To husband out life's taper to the close,
> And keep the flame from wasting by repose.
> And as a hare, whom hounds and horns pursue,
> Pants to the place from whence at first she flew,
> I still had hopes, my long vexations past,
> Here to return, and die at home at last."

And, now, here I am, *free to breathe my native air on my own ground.*

My distinct recollections reach no further back than the close of the revolutionary war. I well remember seeing the disbanded soldiers returning, after the close of it; and I well remember quite a number of aged and venerable men in my neighborhood at that time, who, without doubt, retained the manners, customs, and modes of thinking, of a remote ancestry. There were, besides, four clergymen — one in each of the four parishes — in the ancient town, whose ministry, of sixty years' duration each, was drawing to a close.

Till the close of the revolutionary war, and for some years thereafter, it is not probable that there had been much change in the condition of our forefathers. They were a staid and conservative race. Novelties were looked upon by them with distrust. They were plain and homespun in every thing. Ostentation was far from being a characteristic among them. Each felt safe in treading in the steps of his father before him.

The dwellings of those days were without paint, inside and out; and the churches were in a similar predicament. The furniture of their dwellings was of the simplest kind, though often convenient and comfortable: sofas, stuffed-back and cushion-seated chairs, and carpets, were unknown to them. In their houses you would find —

> "The whitewashed wall, the nicely sanded floor," —

and perhaps —

> "The varnished clock that clicked behind the door;
> The hearth, except when winter chilled the day,
> With aspin-boughs, and flowers and fennel gay."

And in some instances, perhaps, —

> "The broken teacups, wisely kept for show,
> Ranged o'er the chimney, glistened in a row."

And as for music, there was the good old spinning-wheel to be heard in every dwelling, which was suggestive of much that was delightful. It indicated industry and thrift, and gave promise of comfortable clothing; and, what was much better, it was a healthful exercise for the young females: it developed and fortified their energies, gave them freshness and florid beauty, and fitted them to become desirable companions and housewives. Instead of this healthful music, we now have the sickening piano, suggestive of nothing but effeminacy, luxury, and the want of better employment. Our grandmothers were the manufacturers, almost wholly, of the cloth used in their families: of course, they were accustomed to labor, and were real helpmates.

Our ancestors, at the conclusion of the great contest confirming our independence as a nation, having exhausted much of their means in securing that object, were, in some measure, in destitute circumstances. Their circulating medium was reduced almost to nothing. Their paper-money had proved utterly worthless; and it was with much difficulty that specie could be procured to pay their taxes. And those who were in debt found it almost impossible to meet their engagements: economy and frugality, therefore, were, in all their operations, quite indispensable.

I have before remarked, that our ancestors were a plain, homespun people: they were not rich, and scarcely any of them were poor. Their condition was that of mediocrity and equality; so much so, that some of the wags in the neighboring towns, who were inclined to be witty, characterized them by saying, that in Bridgewater there was neither a poor man nor a rich one, a wise man nor a fool.

Our ancestors were, moreover, remarkable for their uniformity and fixedness in matters of religion. During the ministration of the four pastors before alluded to, all within the limits of each parish attended at the same church. It is not known, that, in those days, there was a single dissentient; and the four ministers could freely interchange with each other. People in those days had not begun to split hairs about matters in regard to which no mortal in this life can arrive to any degree of certainty.

There was in those days, in each of the four parishes, as in Goldsmith's favorite village, —

> "The never-failing brook, the busy mill,
> The decent church that topped the neighboring hill."

There was also, in each parish, the good man, of whom he says, —

> "A man he was to all the country dear,
> And passing rich with forty pounds a year:
> Remote from towns he ran his godly race,
> Nor e'er had changed, nor wished to change, his place.
> Unskilful he to fawn, or seek for power,
> By doctrines fashioned to the varying hour;
> Far other aims his heart had learned to prize, —
> More bent to raise the wretched than to rise.
> And as a bird each fond endearment tries
> To tempt its new-fledged offspring to the skies,
> He tried each art, reproved each dull delay,
> Allured to brighter worlds, and led the way."

There was also, in each of the parishes, the place —

> "Where gray-beard mirth and smiling toil retired;
> Where village statesmen talked with looks profound,
> And news much older than their ale went round."

It may, however, have been flip, or good old cider, that went round, instead of ale, in our ancestors' days. Whoever reads Goldsmith's "Deserted Village" will find much that will strikingly apply to the condition of our forefathers.

Our ancestors had another source of enjoyment, in their almost perfect freedom from lawless intrusion. Scarcely any one, in those days, thought it necessary to fasten his doors, and much less his windows, on retiring for the night. Each *sat under his own vine and his own fig-tree, and had none to molest or make him afraid.*

Thus we see that our ancestors were not without their sources of enjoyment. Their almost perfect equality, so conducive to familiar and unrestrained sociability; their undisturbed unanimity in matters of religion; their freedom from fear of the disorderly or thievish midnight intruder; their facilities for obtaining the wholesome comforts of life, without the deteriorating annoyances of luxury, — all seem to have conspired to make their lot as happy as is attainable in this life.

Notwithstanding all which, we are naturally prone to felicitate ourselves in contrasting our condition with theirs. We find our domiciles and churches everywhere glistening inside and out with paint; our furniture of the most costly kind, consisting of mahogany, black walnut, or rosewood, — heavy, massive, and almost immovable; sofas, ottomans, secretaries, and rich cabinet-wares, too numerous to be mentioned; with woollen carpets, rugs, brass fire-sets, and splendid vehicles for transportation. With these our eyes are dazzled, and our imaginations are led astray.

But let us pause, and consider what is really conducive to enjoyment. Who dares now to retire for the night, without fastening his doors and windows? How much of equality of condition is to be met with, so conducive to good fellowship? How is it with regard to religious fellowship? Till the close of the last century, no clergyman was ever settled in either of the four parishes, with one solitary exception, that did not spend his days there. How has it been since? In the old East Parish, now town of East Bridgewater, since the commencement of the present century there have been settled no less than six ministers, five of whom are now living; and there are now in the same town, formerly the East Parish, three other societies, neither of the ministers of which can agree on an exchange with either of the others. And in the other towns, comprising the other parishes of ancient Bridgewater, it is understood that there is, and has been, at least an approximation to the same state of things. Let these considerations cause us to pause, and consider how much, if at all, our condition, as conducive to true enjoyment, is to be preferred, on the whole, to that of our ancestors.

There is, however, one particular in which we may fairly rejoice in a real improvement upon what they enjoyed. Wheeled carriages, for the transportation of persons, they can scarcely be said to have had any. A few, and they were very few, elderly people had rickety old chaises to convey them to meeting. Wagons for the purpose are of recent invention. The horse, saddle, and pillion afforded almost the only means, except when there was sleighing, for the transportation of persons; and such was the case nearly to the close of the last century.

One more quotation from Goldsmith, and this garrulity of an old man shall be brought to a close, at least for the present: —

> "Thus fares the land, by luxury betrayed,
> In nature's simplest charms at first arrayed;
> But, verging to decline, its splendors rise,
> Its vistas strike, its palaces surprise."

May this vaticination never be verified in either of the Bridgewaters, though their *splendors should continue to rise, their vistas strike, their palaces surprise.*

---

2. "*The Commonwealth of Massachusetts.* — May her glory shine as bright in the *preservation* of *liberty, independence,* and *union,* as in the struggles for their acquisition!"

Response by the Band.

3. "*The Chief Justice of Massachusetts.* — He reads upon the tablets of our quiet churchyard the memorials of his ancestors: on the tablets of our hearts he may read our welcome to the descendant."

Hon. LEMUEL SHAW, of Boston, responded substantially as follows: —

MR. PRESIDENT, — For the very kind and significant terms in which you and the very large and respectable assembly here present have noticed myself, as a descendant of a respectable ancestry, I pray you to accept the expression of my heartfelt and sincere thanks. My gratitude for this kind and respectful notice is not the less sincere and personal, when I consider, as I cannot fail to do, that that marked expression of affectionate regard is, to a certain extent, influenced by the honorable and responsible office which I hold in the judiciary of the Commonwealth.

So far as my observation and experience have gone, — and they have been pretty extensive, — I think I may say with truth, that, if there be any one sentiment general, strong, and predominant, amongst the thoughtful and considerate people of Massachusetts, it is an earnest desire to establish and maintain, at all times and under all circumstances, an able, faithful, and impartial administration of justice. Corresponding with this highly salutary principle, I have never failed to observe a general disposition among the people to cherish and express a feeling of affectionate and respectful regard to all those who have held high judicial offices, and who have performed the duties of such offices with a reasonable degree of capacity and fidelity.

We are reminded, sir, by the historical reminiscences so vividly brought to our notice to-day, what indeed we well knew before, that Bridgewater was founded, and commenced her career of advancement and improvement, under the government of the old colony of Plymouth, which became annexed to Massachusetts by the Province Charter of 1692. But although Massachusetts was then comparatively a large community, and the colony of Plymouth a small one, I believe I may say, with truth, that we were not received as a dependency or subordinate community, but were admitted at once to the free participation and enjoyment of all the benefits of the enlarged common government. And I hesitate not to say, that, before and since this union, the inhabitants of the old colony — by military services in defence of the country, by public services in church and state — have done their fair share in advancing the common good and enhancing the common reputation; and I rejoice in adding my belief, that they have received their full share of all the honors and distinctions which it has been in the power of the common parent to bestow. Here, sir, in a sort of family meeting, where nothing is intended to go beyond our own circle, I hope it may not be regarded unwarrantable vanity in alluding to a circumstance calculated to do honor to the land of our birth. May I therefore be pardoned in mentioning, that, soon after I was appointed to the judicial office which I now hold, there was a centennial celebration at Worcester to commemorate the establishment of courts in that county, at which the judges of the Supreme Judicial Court, then in session there, attended to do honor to the occasion? Some one there called attention to the fact, — and so it was, — that, of the four judges of which the Supreme Judicial Court was then composed, three were natives of the old colony.

Mr. President, we are here this day — and, for myself, I rejoice in the happy opportunity to recognize and renew the recollections and associations which bind us together — as the descendants of a common ancestry, and to congratulate each other upon the striking manifestations of success, prosperity, and social improvement, which surround and pervade the place of our common origin. Here, from one small settlement, we behold the establishment of four large, thriving, and well-ordered communities, each with its various churches, academies, and schools; its numerous farms and commodious dwellings; its manufactories, and places of trade; and each numbering its inhabitants by thousands, enjoying all the advantages which religious and civil institutions cannot fail to bestow. And all this has occurred upon a scene and over a territory, — as we have been reminded by the interesting historical researches through which the orator has to-day vividly carried us, — a territory "inhabited," shall I say? — no, scarcely more than wandered over, — by a handful of savages, little raised above the rank of barbarism.

And within what time has this vast and beneficial change taken place? In certain points of view, two hundred years may appear to be a long period of time; to each man's personal experience, looking at the events of his own life only, it may seem so: but, in marking the infancy, growth, and maturity of tribes, states, and nations, it is, in truth, a comparatively short period. Not only Bridgewater and the old colony, but this vast confederacy of the North-American States, have risen to their present greatness in the short space of two hundred years. May I, in this connection, be permitted to allude to a circumstance, somewhat curious in itself, which may aid the imagination in conceiving of, and realizing the comparative shortness of, this time? We all know, from well-authenticated tradition, that Peregrine White was the first child born in the Plymouth colony; that his birth, therefore, was at about 1620; and that he lived to be about eighty-five years old, thus carrying him to about 1705. Mr. Cobb, the centenarian of Kingston, died in 1803, at the age of a hundred and seven. Perhaps some who hear me may recollect him. I myself visited him at the commencement of the present century. He stated that he recollected Peregrine White, and had seen him, and had heard him talk. And this might even be; for he must have been eight or ten years old when Peregrine White died. Paradoxical as it may seem, Mr. Cobb lived through part of three centuries, — the seventeenth, eighteenth, and nineteenth. Born in 1696, and dying in 1803, he lived four years in the seventeenth, during the whole of the eighteenth, and three years in the nineteenth century. Thus three lives, one, at least, still subsisting, — and probably many others, some of whom now hear me, — cover the whole period from the arrival of the " Mayflower " to the present time.

What, then, we are led to inquire, with earnest and affectionate interest, led to this change from a wilderness to a garden, from barbarism to high civilization? These causes, these results, were probably not peculiar to the founders of the old colony; but then they were strikingly displayed and illustrated.

In the first place, the founders were actuated and governed, in all their thoughts and all their movements, by high religious and moral principle. They were not adventurers, who had left their country for a time to mend their fortunes, and then return to pass the residue of their lives in their native land: they came to seek an abiding-place, to establish a home for themselves and their descendants, which should satisfy their cherished ideas of a pure, religious commonwealth. They came with little property; but the means on which they relied, — and on which, as the event proved, they might rely with success, — next to an undoubting faith in the providence of God, were earnest minds and willing hands.

To establish the means of religious instruction and public worship, where all might participate and enjoy equal privileges, was regarded as a duty of the first necessity. But their religious character has been too often considered to require any extended comment now. Their views may often have been narrow or erroneous; they may have been stiff, or even obstinate, in maintaining them: but they were sincere. It is not on their religious character, however, that I would dwell; but I do wish to ask your attention to their high moral principles. In my judgment, they were truly and conscientiously governed by a principle of strict integrity, a pure sense of exact justice, of strict equality of rights in the distribution and enjoyment of all civil and social benefits and advantages. If a tract of land was granted to a company of proprietors, it was to those who had united to form a settlement, designed for their personal occupation, and divided with strict equality, usually by lot; and if, by any accident or mistake, any one had not his full share in real value, it was made up to him out of the common stock. No seignories, no large tracts, were granted out to individuals for speculation and for being leased, or for the purpose of creating distinctions in rank or social position; and I have always regarded it as one of the vast advantages, and as giving a character in the outset to the condition of society, that land was granted in small parcels to actual settlers, to be held by actual occupants, by the freest of all tenures. This affords the highest encouragement to permanent improvement; because every occupant feels assured that every permanent improvement will enure to his own benefit and that of his children. This it is which converts the sterile plain into a fertile field; this it is which marks the distinction in improvement between the farms and buildings of a body of free yeomanry, cultivating their own lands, and the farms and buildings of a tenantry, even on the most fertile soil.

But next to the religious character of our ancestors, and the high-toned, strong sense of morality, of justice and integrity, of perfect equality of rights, which marked their conduct in all their social and political dealings and relations with each other, I consider that the remarkable growth of the communities, in advancing from poverty to competency, to wealth, and to all the refinements of an advanced civilization, are mainly attributable to two qualities, — industry and frugality. Labor, honest labor, even hard and persevering labor, in a laudable and honest calling, brought no discouragement, no want of respect, no loss of social position. This was a general and pervading feeling, and extended to all classes of society. It extended to both sexes: mothers and daughters, as well as fathers and sons, were actuated alike by a common self-devotion to useful industry, to advance the common interests of the family. If a son was to be supported at college, or a daughter to be fitted out with a comfortable marriage provision, it was only a stimulus to more assiduous and cheerful industry to the whole household.

But I fear I am detaining you too long. I do wish, however, at the hazard of being tedious, in reference to the last topic alluded to, to express, for myself and my cotemporaries of the present time, a deep feeling of gratitude, veneration, and filial affection, for our female ancestors. Though less conspicuous, their duties were not less important and efficient. Animated by an abiding sense of religious dependence, and sustained by an unshaken faith; governed by an entire devotion to duty, and in a self-sacrificing spirit; without display, and without a thought of being applauded or noticed, — they proceeded in the performance of their appropriate duties with a quiet but persevering energy, which did much to mould the character of their sons and daughters to honor and virtue, and elevate the tone of society by impressing it with something of their own pure and lofty spirit.

These virtues and characteristics were not rare, exceptional, and occasional, but everywhere abounded as the leading characteristics of the wives and mothers of our early ancestors, and tended to give to society formed under domestic auspices a character of high excellence, though still little advanced in wealth. Wealth is adventitious: virtue is perennial.

And may we not, with propriety, hold up these virtues of the wives and mothers of the olden time, as objects worthy of imitation by the women of our own age? For although they are now seldom called on to engage in the same labors; though the useful arts of domestic manufacture have given place to literature, the fine arts, and the more delicate occupations of refined society; though the music of the piano has superseded that of the spinning-wheel, — yet the same piety and faith, the same disinterested, self-sacrificing devotion to duty, the same quiet energy and earnest maternal affection, which constituted the crowning grace of the humble dwellings of our ancestors, will still add grace and dignity, and shed a purifying influence upon the more sumptuous habitations and refined households of modern society.

Permit me to offer you a sentiment: —

"May each succeeding Centennial Anniversary witness the same deep interest in the homes of our ancestors, the love and veneration of their virtues, and the same fraternal harmony, which this day characterize the re-union of the Bridgewaters."

---

4. "*The Orator of the Day.* — A descendant of one of the original proprietors and settlers of Bridgewater: no long line of ancestry can add to his reputation as a *statesman* and a *man*."

Mr. WASHBURN, in responding to the above sentiment, said that he had already taxed their indulgence too severely this day to feel justified in occupying any more of their time, which could be so much more profitably employed in listening to others.

But he should be doing injustice to his own feelings, if he suffered the occasion to pass without expressing the satisfaction with which he had this day visited a spot so long associated in his mind as the early home of his ancestors.

He had come here well-nigh a stranger; but as one object after another had been pointed out to him, and he had looked upon the farms which had been planted by men of his own name two centuries ago, he felt as if he had come back to what he had a right to claim as his own home.*

---

* Ellis Ames, Esq., presented the speaker, on this occasion, an original parchment-deed, executed by John Washburn, 2d, one of the original settlers of the town, bearing date, Nov. 1, 1686, and acknowledged before William Bradford, Deputy-Governor.

And, when he found himself greeted with the warm welcome of hospitality, he forgot that his birthplace was anywhere than amidst these scenes of comfort and independence by which they were surrounded.

But he claimed the right of a stranger to speak, as an impartial observer, of what he had witnessed this day; and he did not hesitate to say, that nowhere could we look for a higher degree of intelligence, good order, and, in every sense of the term, respectability, than the multitude who had convened here had this day evinced.

Here were assembled, promiscuously, the people of four independent communities, numbering by thousands, and yet observing all the decorum and self-respect which are looked for in the social gatherings of friends and familiar associates, the courtesies of social life controlling the scenes of a public festive holiday.

Nor was it too much to say, that they witnessed in this the legitimate fruits of the opinions, institutions, and example which had been left to this generation by their fathers.

Well might Bridgewater be proud of such sons and daughters; and well might they come up hither, from their homes far and near, to do honor to the memory of its founders, and the associations that cluster around this spot.

He proposed, as a sentiment, —

"Bridgewater and her Children. — May she ever find a devotion as sincere on their part, and they a home as prosperous and a welcome as cordial on hers, as the old homestead has this day presented!"

---

5. "*The Attorney-General of the Commonwealth.* — Elected to his office for the *ability* and *fidelity* with which he has discharged its duties, and *not* for *party* purposes."

Hon. JOHN H. CLIFFORD, the Attorney-General of the Commonwealth, who had attended the celebration, and would have replied to this toast, was compelled to leave the table, by pressing official engagements, before it was announced; leaving with a friend the following sentiment, which was read and cordially received: —

"The Ancient Town of Bridgewater. — She has successfully solved the most difficult political problem of modern times, by showing that there can be a North and a South, an East and a West, whose lines of division only serve 'to form a more perfect Union.'"

---

6. "*The Ancient Ministers of the Town.* — Keith, Perkins, and Reed, of the West; Shaw and Sanger, of the South; the two Angiers, of the East; and Porter, of the North, — in their times, the *beacon-lights* of *knowledge*, the *heralds* of *religious* and *civil liberty*. Their remains rest peacefully beneath our soil; the hallowed influence of their lives and labors, diffused throughout the community, will never *die*."

Rev. RALPH SANGER, of Dover, replied substantially as follows: —

MR. PRESIDENT, — You will bear me witness that I knew nothing of this sentiment till late last evening. Another person (Dr. Gannett, of Boston), an honored descendant of Bridgewater, was expected to respond to this sentiment. He is not here. I was asked to take his place. My feelings prompted me to do it. I could not bear the thought that there should be no response to this sentiment; for although delicacy may forbid me to say much of *one* whose name is mentioned in the sentiment just read, yet several of them I had seen, and of all of them I had read or heard.

Mr. President, most of the early ministers of Bridgewater attained a great age. The average length of the ministry of Keith, Perkins, and Reed, was the remarkably long period of fifty-six years. The average length of the ministry of the first Angier, Shaw, and Porter, was the still longer period of more than sixty-one years. This fact reflects much credit both upon the ministers and the people. It shows that there was mutual attachment, without which a ministry can be neither long nor profitable. It furnishes a striking contrast to the frequent changes in the ministry at the present time. I know that some religious societies have had not less than six, and others not less than eight, ministers since the time of my ordination. A brother clergyman, in reference to this state of things, remarked, that soon a minister would be considered *very old* at the age of twenty-five, and that people would wish to get a *young* and *smart* man to take his place.

Mr. President, I saw, in my early years, the venerable Shaw and Porter. They sustained, each of them, a long and useful ministry. They were beloved in life, and lamented in death. Their children and children's children have risen up, and called them blessed. They are honored in many of their descendants, and surely, in no small degree, by two of them present on this occasion, whose voices we have been glad this day to hear, — one presiding with dignity at this table; and the other presiding, with eminent ability, as Chief Justice of the Supreme Court of our honored Commonwealth.

But, Mr. President, the two ministers just mentioned died when I was very young. Dr. Reed, on the other hand, survived till I had seen more than twoscore years. I knew him from my earliest recollection. He was often at my father's house. He and my father were like brothers. They loved each other; they respected each other; they frequently visited each other; they often exchanged on the sabbath; they preached for each other the lecture preparatory to communion; so that I often heard him both in public and in private. He was very interesting and instructive in conversation. Dr. Reed, as it seems to me, was an *original thinker*. I have known ministers who would probably be regarded as more learned; I have known those who perhaps had a knowledge of more languages, and were esteemed more critical scholars: but I think that I have never known a minister who had a more original and discriminating mind. Judge Metcalf said of him, that he reminded him of Franklin. Like Franklin, he had an original mind; he uttered short and pithy sayings; thoughts came out of his mind like sparks of the electric fluid from the battery; they came not only with *light,* but with power. Let me add, that his character was no less remarkable for its excellence than his mind was for its clearness.

> " His doctrine and his life,
> Coincident, exhibit lucid proof
> That he was honest in the sacred cause."

Mr. President, there is one minister, mentioned in the sentiment, of whose life and character and services I may not speak at large. But I may be allowed to state one or two facts to show that he was a patron of literature, and a lover of "religious and civil liberty." Though his salary was small, he expended freely of his little income to purchase books, and collected, during his lifetime, what was thought to be not only the largest, but the most valuable, library in that vicinity. He paid nearly a whole year's salary for one single work; viz., "Rees's Cyclopædia." He contributed *one-thirtieth part* toward the first academy which was erected in Bridgewater. He was very fond of literary and scientific, as well as theological, studies; and, whenever occasion required, he stood forth the defender of "religious and civil liberty."

Mr. President, I have spoken briefly of the "ancient ministers of Bridgewater" whom I have seen, and of whom I have personal knowledge. Those whom I have not seen — the venerable Keith and Perkins and Angier, of whom history and tradition speak — were doubtless "beacon-lights" in their day and generation. They performed a good work in their time. They sowed seed, which has sprung up, and borne precious fruit, of which we and all coming after us will partake. Sir, I concur heartily in the closing language of the sentiment, — "The hallowed influence of their lives and labors, diffused through the community, will never die." No, sir, it will not die. Let us hope that it will live and flourish; let us hope and pray that the good influence, which has come from our fathers to us, may be like a pure and holy stream, widening and deepening and increasing in all future time. And so, when the children of the ancient town of Bridgewater shall come in 1956, from "the North and the South, the East and the West," to the *Third Centennial Anniversary*, may they come with as *warm* and *joyous* hearts as we do *this day!*

Mr. President, allow me, before I close, to say that I am here to-day in the *home* of my early years, in the *home* of my childhood and youth, in the *home* of my *earliest memories* and *affections*. I rejoice to be here. I rejoice to see the family at home so much enlarged and improved; to see so many new brothers and sisters in the "old homestead." God bless them all, and multiply them a thousand-fold!

Mr. President, permit me to close by offering the following sentiment: —

"The children of Bridgewater, who have been abroad, and have been kindly invited to return home, present their hearty thanks for the generous hospitality which they have received in the 'old homestead.'"

---

7. "*The Judiciary of Massachusetts*, — the anchor which holds the Ship of State fast to her moorings, whatever storms may assail her."

Hon. GEORGE P. SANGER, one of the Judges of the Court of Common Pleas, being called upon to respond, spoke, in substance, as follows: —

I regret, Mr. President, for your sake, and for that of the brothers and sisters before us, that it had not fallen to him to respond to this sentiment whose name instantly occurs to every one, as the profound lawyer, and the most able, learned, and upright judge, whenever, in our Commonwealth, the judiciary is referred to, and who, present here as a descendant of one of the former worthies of the town, has already answered to a sentiment complimentary to himself. But his presence makes my duty light; for my best response to the sentiment to which you have done me the honor to ask me to reply is simply to point you to him, who, throughout the Commonwealth, is known and honored as the upright and honorable man, and, over the nation and across the ocean, is recognized and appreciated as the learned and profound judge.

You will permit me, Mr. President, to make one suggestion in regard to the phraseology of the sentiment. It speaks of the Ship of State only as at her moorings, and assigns to the judiciary the sphere of holding her to her moorings, whatever storms may assail her. This is all true, sir. But our Ship of State is not always at her moorings: she has her voyage to accomplish; and, whether her course leads her beneath sunny skies or over stormy seas, the judiciary plays its necessary and important part equally as in holding her to her moorings. For, sir, I believe in that true progress, that steady advance with no backward step, majestic as the march of the ages, by which commonwealths, as well as individuals, are led forward in their upward and onward course. Did I not so believe, the times upon which we have fallen would be to me most grievous; and the incidents of the past few weeks, still fresh in the hearts of the people, would overwhelm me with unutterable sorrow. The low wail of liberty that comes up to us from the Federal Capitol, where freedom of speech is stricken down in what should be her sanctuary; and the agonizing shrieks that pierce our ears from the Western prairies, where the sons and daughters of the Free States are insulted, oppressed, outraged, and murdered, simply because they would keep that fair garden of the world open to freedom, — would burden me to the earth, did I not believe, that, even now, a brighter day is beginning to dawn, and that the historian of American liberty will look upon this year as the time when, and these acts as the crowning aggressions by which, the free people of the nation were at last to be aroused to the determination, that thenceforward, for ever, the blight of slavery should not be extended. And, sir, may not this be one of the lessons that this time and occasion teach? Looking forth upon these fair fields, which our fathers, with unremitting toil, redeemed from the wilderness, should we not pledge ourselves anew to lives of honorable and manly labor? Standing by the sods that rest lightly upon their honored dust, let us dedicate ourselves for the future to a life, as nearly as may be, as patient, as enduring, as frugal, as honest, as patriotic, as Christian, and so as fruitful, as theirs. Living in a land by them made free, let us consecrate ourselves for ever as untiring champions of religious freedom and republican liberty.

In the Appendix, Mr. President, to Mitchell's "History of Bridgewater," which has been referred to so often and so favorably to-day, there is a preface, written by the Mathers, of religious memory, to a published sermon of, I think, the Rev. Mr. Keith, the first minister of this town, in which they speak of the then reputation of Bridgewater as that of " a most pious and a most praying town; " and to the piety and prayers of its people do they attribute the many mercies which God had vouchsafed to them. I give you, sir, as a sentiment: —

"The most praying and most pious town of Bridgewater: May its descendants imitate the example of their ancestors! and so to themselves insure the great reward."

---

8. "*The Adopted Children of our Common Mother.* — We extend to them the hand of fellowship, and welcome them to all the blessings and privileges of our common inheritance."

Hon. WILLIAM BAYLIES, of West Bridgewater, responded as follows: —

MR. PRESIDENT, — I shall not attempt to make what might properly be called a speech. Such an attempt would require an effort beyond my strength, both of body and mind. I must, therefore, in replying to the toast just offered, restrict myself to narrow limits and a few words.

To be recognized, on this occasion and in this presence, as an adopted son of Bridgewater, — Old Bridgewater, in all her territorial entireness and integrity, — is gratifying to my feelings: nothing could be more so. I acknowledge the relationship, and am proud of it. Old Bridgewater I shall never forget: the remembrance of her is dear to my heart, and will be so till that heart shall become as cold as marble.

And though I was not born within her limits, and though my life-blood does not "track its parent lake" through her first or early settlers or their descendants, yet I believe that I appreciate the merits and services of those good and true men as justly and as highly, that I respect and venerate their characters as much, and that I join in this celebration, intended to revive, to honor, and perpetuate their memory, as cordially, as though I had been a native of the soil of Old Bridgewater, and my cradle had been rocked within her limits.

The founders of Bridgewater were men of no ordinary stamp. Though sorely beset and severely tried, yet, with unflinching fortitude, surmounting all obstacles, and throwing off all encumbrances, they accomplished their purpose; they laid the foundation of a great town, — a princely municipality. They were men of enlarged minds and a wise policy. Appreciating the value of knowledge, they provided liberally, considering their means, for the education of their children. Knowing the vital importance of religion to states, communities, and individuals, they made liberal provision, as far as their ability would admit, for the maintenance of public worship and the preaching of the gospel.

Old Bridgewater was highly favored and blessed in her clergymen; and, when they passed away, she lost some of the "most precious jewels of her coronet." It is not my purpose, nor am I qualified, to speak their praises; but of one with whom I was intimately acquainted, and who honored me with his friendship, I must be indulged in a more particular notice. I refer to the late Dr. John Reed, who was the minister of the Old West Parish when I came here fifty-seven years ago.

He was a man of plain, simple, unaffected manners, with a heart free from all guile; of great sensibility, and overflowing with the milk of human kindness; but possessed of a strong mind, and of great reasoning powers. He was very familiar with the Scriptures, and a learned expounder of their doctrines, and of the great principles of Christianity. He was not called a brilliant preacher, holding very cheap all the arts of rhetoric: but he certainly was an effective, and, I think, an eloquent preacher; for he convinced the judgment by the force of his argument, and penetrated and subdued the heart by the pathos of his delivery.

But he had merit higher than this. What he preached to others he practised himself. His doctrines were exemplified in his life and conversation.

> "His preaching much, but more his practice, wrought
> A living sermon of the truths he taught."

This, I know, is a slight and feeble tribute to the memory of a great and good man; but it is sincere, and comes from the heart.

I will now conclude with a few words addressed particularly to those who are here from the four Bridgewaters. We all know that Old Bridgewater no longer exists as a corporation, except in contemplation of law. She has been dismembered, — divided into four towns, separated from each other by distinct and independent organizations. This separation is fixed, and will remain. Re-union is not desired, and, if it were, would be hardly practicable. But still there may be a union, not created by law, but a voluntary union, — a union of hearts, irrespective of town lines and town organizations, but not conflicting with them, nor interfering with them, — a union formed and supported by social and friendly intercourse, and by a disposition to promote the interests and happiness of each other. By cultivating this friendly and Christian spirit, the four Bridgewaters will remain united in the best sense of the word, and be Old Bridgewater still; and I say, from the bottom of my heart, Old Bridgewater for ever!

---

9. "*Those who have practised the Healing Art in the Ancient Town of Bridgewater, or can trace their Descent therefrom.* — Skilful in the prevention and cure of disease, each of them, like an apostle of old, may well be called 'the beloved physician.'"

Dr. EBENEZER ALDEN, of Randolph, replied substantially as follows: —

MR. PRESIDENT, — I thank you for your kind personal notice, and especially for your high compliment to the profession of which I am a member.

I cannot feel myself to be a stranger here to-day. Of the five generations which have intervened between myself and the stripling who first leaped upon Plymouth Rock, and who was the last male survivor of the "Mayflower," four were inhabitants of Bridgewater.

Joseph, second son of Hon. John Alden, of Duxbury, was a proprietor in his father's right, and came here as early as 1656. He was much respected, and received the title of *Goodman*, as your town-records show. He died, in 1697, at the age of seventy-three; and his remains were, without doubt, deposited in the ancient burying-ground, but the exact place of his sepulture knoweth no man of this generation. Could his descendants of the present day do a more fitting thing than to erect a plain monument to his memory?

Joseph Alden, son of Joseph, was a resident in the south precinct, and an officer in the church there; where he died, at the age of eighty, in 1747. Then followed in succession two Daniels; one the husband, the other a son, of Abigail, daughter of Judith Shaw, whose character has just been so graphically delineated by her great-grandson, Hon. Lemuel Shaw, Chief Justice of the Commonwealth. They were both good men and true; residents in Bridgewater for a time, but finally removed, — one to find a resting-place in Stafford, Conn.; the other in Lebanon, N.H. I may add, that, like their fathers, they enjoyed not only the blessing of the upper and the nether springs, but, according to the promise, an abundant heritage of children; and that, with rare exceptions, they have honored the memory and training of their sires.

My father settled as a physician in the immediate vicinity of Bridgewater in 1781, and for many years was in habits of frequent — I had almost said daily — intercourse with its inhabitants; and, for nearly half a century since his death, the kindness to the father has not been withholden from the son. My interest in these scenes, therefore, Mr. President, is similar to your own. I thank you again for an invitation to visit the old domicile, and to unite with you in celebrating a common ancestry.

But, sir, in the sentiment to which I have been invited to respond, you allude to the medical profession; and I thank you for the allusion. Next to the Christian ministry, I maintain that there is no more useful or honorable calling than that of the good physician. He is with you from the cradle to the grave; from the first struggle into life, through all its morbid changes, to its close. He is an inmate of your families and firesides, — in the hour of peril, to ward off danger; to call back the ebbing tide of life, when each pulsation is apprehended to be the last; to restore the wife to the embraces of her husband, and the child to the bosom of its mother; and by his assiduity and skill, and the blessing of God upon his efforts, to send joy and gladness into hearts stricken and oppressed with emotions which no language can express. And, when he can do nothing more, he stands by your dying pillow, a sympathizing, sorrowing friend, to mitigate, as far as he may, the pains of separation between the departing spirit and its earthy tenement.

Such was Samuel Fuller, one of the company who landed in Plymouth in 1620, the first physician in New England, — first in the order of time, and a model physician in character. For twelve years he went in and out among the people; like a guardian angel, making all happy with whom he associated. He was frequently requested to extend his labors beyond the boundaries of Plymouth Colony and the neighboring Indian tribes. Twice — viz., in 1628 and 1629 — he visited Salem, by desire of Governor Endicott, during the prevalence of severe sickness among the newly arrived immigrants; and his efforts were attended with the most gratifying success. In a letter to Governor Bradford, bearing date June 28, 1630, he says, "I have been to Mattapan (Dorchester), and have let some twenty of those people blood." But Dr. Fuller was eminent not only in his profession, but in other walks of life. Before he left Holland, he had been chosen an officer in Robinson's church. His judgment in ecclesiastical affairs was highly valued. He was a wise counsellor, a faithful friend, a zealous and consistent Christian. Too soon for the church and for his country, he was called to go up higher. He died of epidemic fever in 1633; and the people " mourned with a great and very sore lamentation."

From that time to the present, the Old Colony has had a succession of physicians, who, if they have not all attained the eminence of Samuel Fuller, have adorned their profession, and secured the respect of their contemporaries.

Time would fail me to present a catalogue of their names,

much more the briefest sketch of their characters. They are embalmed in the memories of a grateful posterity, and have an imperishable monument in your hearts.

Many of the early ministers in the Old Colony practised medicine as well as preached the gospel; not intending by this to obtrude themselves into the business of the regular physician, or, as quaint Sir Thomas Browne has it, "to chase two hares at one time," but as a necessity in the absence of more efficient helpers. Such were Rev. Charles Chauncy, at Scituate; Rev. Samuel Brown, at Abington; Rev. John Shaw, of Bridgewater; and others.

Thomas and Comfort Starr, Matthew Fuller, Samuel Seabury, Thomas Little, and Francis Le Baron, were reputable physicians and chirurgeons in Plymouth and the vicinity at an early day. In later times, we find the names of Bryant, Hitchcock, Otis, Lathrop, Winslow, Crane, Carver, Shaw, Thaxter, Thacher, and many more; some of whom, in the revolutionary contest, were distinguished as patriots as well as physicians.

In the immediate place of our assembling, we call to mind, in succession, the names of Howard, Perkins, Dunbar, and Whitman; the latter a personal friend of my own, as well as of many who hear me. They and their associates were noble men, worthy of the times in which they lived, and of the reputation they secured; and they have left to their successors an example which may be safely imitated.

Allow me, Mr. President, in conclusion, to propose the following sentiment: —

"Our Puritan ancestors and their immediate descendants, the first settlers of Bridgewater. They appreciated moral worth in all the departments of society. The best tribute we can offer to their memories is to cherish their principles, and to transmit them, with the institutions they originated, to coming generations."

10. "*The Memory of Nahum Mitchell, the Historian of Bridgewater,*—an honor to the science of sacred music; an upright judge; and a faithful legislator, both of the State and nation. His untiring industry, in rescuing from oblivion the memorials of the past, deserves the gratitude of succeeding generations."

The following notice of Judge Mitchell was submitted by Hon. AARON HOBART, of East Bridgewater:—

The above sentiment is one most fitting for the occasion. He whom it commemorates was distinguished by a long life, — a large portion of it spent in the practice of an honorable profession, and in the service of his country. It was my good fortune, more than fifty years ago, to enter his office as a law student, and reside in his family. From that time to his sudden death in Plymouth, where he had gone to join in celebrating the two hundred and thirty-third anniversary of the embarkation of the Pilgrim Fathers at Delft Haven, I have known and held him, as all who knew him did, in great respect.

Judge Mitchell was a descendant, in the fourth degree, from Experience Mitchell, who came to Plymouth in the third ship, the "Ann," in 1623. He was the son of Cushing Mitchell, and Jennet, his wife, who was a daughter of Hugh Orr, of Bridgewater, but a native of Lochwinnoch, in Scotland, and was born Feb. 12, 1769. Having been fitted by Beza Hayward, of Bridgewater, he entered Harvard College in 1785, and graduated in course, in 1789, with what reputation for scholarship is not known; but his accuracy in matters of scholarship in after-life would seem to render it certain that he could have been no mean proficient. His part at Commencement was a syllogistic disputation, with Asaph Churchill, on the thesis, "*Gravitas non est essentialis materiæ proprietas.*" After leaving college, he read law with the late John Davis, of Plymouth, afterwards Judge of the United States District Court; was admitted to the bar in November, 1792; and, soon after, opened an office in his native place.

He soon atracted attention in his profession; and the estimation in which he was held by the public, and by those who had the appointing power in the State, appears in the many offices which were from time to time conferred upon him.

He was nine years a representative in the General Court, — seven from Bridgewater, and two from Boston; a member of the eighth Congress of the United States; senator from Plymouth County from 1813 to 1814; and a member of the Executive Council from 1814 to 1820. On the abolition of the old County Court of Common Pleas, and the establishment of a Circuit Court of Common Pleas in 1811, he, though not of the same political party with the ruling power, was appointed one of the justices of the new court for the southern circuit, comprehending the counties of Plymouth, Bristol, and Barnstable, and, on the resignation of Thomas B. Adams, succeeded him as Chief Justice. In 1822, he was chosen State Treasurer, and held the office for five consecutive years. Besides these offices, he received appointments under special commissions. He was appointed, with Edward H. Robbins, of Milton, and Nicholas Tillinghast, of Taunton, in 1801, to settle a disputed boundary-line between Massachusetts and Rhode Island; and in 1823, with Mr. Robbins, and George Bliss, of Springfield, to settle the line between Massachusetts and Connecticut. His last appointment was chairman of the first commission for exploring the country from Boston to Albany for a railroad.*

The performance of the various duties of these high and responsible offices was confided to competent and safe hands. Judge Mitchell was a man of great industry, quickness of perception, and caution, and united to a discriminating judgment the attentiveness and precision of the mathematician. His habits of inquiry were so remarkable, that he was never satisfied with investigation, nor desisted from it, so long as

* Judge Mitchell was also an active member of the Massachusetts Historical Society.

he had less than all the light he could obtain on the subject. He was a man that did, and did well, whatever he undertook.

As a lawyer, he was distinguished for sound learning, and fair and honorable practice. The late Chief Justice Parsons, not long before his death, at an evening-party in Plymouth, one of whom was the venerable and reverend Dr. Kendall, when the name of Nahum Mitchell was mentioned, "spoke of him freely as a man and lawyer. He said it would be improper to draw comparisons between him and other gentlemen of the Old-Colony bar. There were, some of them, very respectable; but certainly Mr. Mitchell was among the very best, and that no one was more accurate and discriminating. He had been in the way of witnessing his accuracy and discernment, having been frequently associated with him in the same cause. He spoke of him for a quarter of an hour in a strain of high encomium."

His qualifications as a lawyer made him a good judge; and such he was generally esteemed. It was, indeed, sometimes said of him that he lacked promptness and decision. This, however, was only in appearance: the opinion probably arose from a desire on his part to do right, which led him to defer judgment until the scales of justice ceased to vibrate, and he could see a clear preponderance.

He was in Congress but for one term. There, he was in a small minority, and did not participate much, if any, in debate, but gave close attention to the business of the house, particularly such as related to matters of finance, and was active and influential on commitees.

The principal measures discussed and acted on while he was a member were — an amendment of the Constitution, requiring the electors of President to name, on distinct ballots, the persons voted for as President and Vice-President; the impeachment of Judge Chase; and the purchase of Louisiana from France. On all these questions, he, with a majority of the Massachusetts delegation, voted in the negative, — against the last because he had a doubt (in which Mr. Jefferson, the

President, participated, but yielded to the pressure of circumstances) of the right of the treaty-making power, under the Constitution, to buy territory to be admitted into the Union as a State, and also because of an uncertainty as to our title under the treaty of cession.

After attending to all his official duties and correspondence, he found himself with many leisure hours on hand. These he employed in reading classic authors, among them Ovid's "Epistolæ Heroidum," in the original, — an interesting book, which he "found, in a bookstore in Georgetown, stowed away among a heap of second-hand volumes;" in translating the works of Horace into English verse; and writing an interesting and amusing poem, in one canto, called the "Indian Pudding." He rarely engaged in any amusement, except an evening game of chess with Samuel W. Dana, a member of Congress from Connecticut; "in which," he said in a letter to a relative, "I am generally conqueror, and have therefore become more skilful than my teacher."

He was a great lover of music, and, from youth to old age, studied it as a science. More than fifty years ago, he commenced the publication of the "Bridgewater Collection of Sacred Music," of which he was the principal editor, although his name never appeared in the titlepage. The work passed through nearly thirty editions, and rendered essential service in improving the then-existing style of music, by substituting, for tunes that were neither dignified, solemn, or decent, such as were chaste, classical, and sufficiently simple to be adapted to the wants of a worshipping assembly. Many pieces of his composition obtained a wide-spread circulation, and were generally performed, — among them, an anthem, called "Lord's Day," and a piece, of several quarto pages, beginning with the words, "Jesus shall reign." He also published a series of articles in the "Boston Musical Gazette," on the history of music, and wrote a treatise on harmony, which a competent judge said, if published, "would have done him no discredit."

The success of his efforts for reform were extensively visible, and especially in the church, where he was a constant worshipper. There he was one of the choir for more than a quarter of a century; and assisted by his relative, the late Bartholomew Brown, who was pre-eminent for the power and excellence of his voice, and the late Rev. Dr. James Flint, for fourteen years the minister of the parish, and others, he trained it to a degree of perfection in psalmody rarely equalled, and gave it an impulse in the right direction, that is felt to the present day.

He was much of an antiquarian, as is evinced by his well-written "History of Bridgewater," which is a monument to his memory that will endure for centuries, and, it may be hoped, as long as the art of printing. That was a work of vast labor. Its numerous scattered materials were to be searched for and gathered up from the state, county, town, church, and family records, and other sources, and reduced to a system. This he did with great care, good judgment, and accuracy, — considering the peculiar liability to mistakes in a work of the kind; and has thus furnished the people of the Bridgewaters with a household book, valuable now and hereafter as a repository of historical and genealogical facts most interesting to them and their posterity.

His private character is a model for imitation. He was affable and familiar; his manners were simple and easy; his temper gentle, even, and cheerful; and his whole deportment such as to inspire confidence and respect. Hospitality reigned in his house; and cheerfulness beamed from his countenance on his happy family, and was reflected back by them. He was eminently a man of peace, and, all his life long, exerted a peculiarly happy faculty he had to promote it in his own neighborhood, and elsewhere within the sphere of his influence. He had faults, — and who has not? — but none which should enter into a candid estimation of his character.

It has been said to be as difficult to compare great men as

great rivers. Some we admire for one thing, and some for another; and we cannot bring them together to measure their exact difference. But taking into the account, as well as we may, all the various talents and acquirements that combine to make up the whole man, I think it may be justly said, without being invidious, that the old town of Bridgewater, though numbering among her sons many eminent men, has never produced his superior.

He has now passed away, full of years and full of honors; but his genial face, his tall, erect, dignified person, and elastic step, will not soon fade from the eyes of those who knew him. Nor will the remembrance of his life be limited to the days of his contemporaries: another generation will keep his memory green.

---

11. "*To the Emigrants from Bridgewater*, who have returned with their descendants to unite with us this day in commemorating the memory and virtues of our forefathers, we bid a most hearty welcome."

12. "*Public Schools*, — the Archimedean lever which moves the world."

13. "*Duxbury*, — the honored mother of Bridgewater. Though her children wandered thus far into the wilderness to plant the first inland town, they look back with affection to the *Gurnet Light*."

Hon. SETH SPRAGUE, of Duxbury, responded as follows : —

MR. PRESIDENT, — After listening to the interesting and eloquent address of Governor Washburn, the pleasing poem of Mr. Reed, and entertained with eloquence, wit, and humor for four long hours, it is only to inflict pain and punishment on the audience for you to call on any one to speak at this late hour. A speaker, who could interest an audience thus satiated with good things, must have power equal to a galvanic battery that would stir the dead. On my own account, I would not utter a single word; but, as Bridgewater is an offspring of Duxbury, I merely respond to the relation, and say, that when Bridgewater, or perhaps a larger territory than was assigned her, was purchased from Massasoit, her whole territory, large as it was, was valued at seven coats of a yard and a half each, nine hatchets, eight hoes, twenty knives, four moose-skins, and ten and a half yards of cotton cloth, — the whole not worth more than twenty-five dollars. Such was the town valued at by the possessors, after a long period of occupation by savage tribes, and, from experience, was not destined to be increased in value by their mode of life, had they possessed it until the present time. Peopled by a civilized, Christian people, in the short space of two hundred years, the value of this same territory is more than five millions current money. Duxbury had the advantage of Bridgewater, in being settled some fifteen years earlier; yet Bridgewater has outstripped her in population and wealth. I am astonished when comparing their statistics. In 1790, Bridgewater had more population than Duxbury and Plymouth, the territory of Plymouth being nearly equal to that of Bridgewater. At the present time, the population of Old Bridgewater is fifty per cent more than Duxbury and Plymouth together. The superior local advantages of Duxbury — situated on the seaboard, with all the advantages of coasting, foreign trade, ship-building, the facilities of transportation, the fisheries, and inducements to enterprise and expansion — render the superiority of Bridgewater the more to her credit. You must, for the first century at least, and probably the first half of the second, have been mainly confined to the cultivation of the soil. I cannot call to mind any place, with no greater local advantages, that has advanced with equal rapidity. The soil of your township is probably superior to any town in Plymouth County. As much behind you as we are, we rejoice at your success and prosperity. You have a right to be proud of your position. I would say more, but ought not to have said so much. I will close with a sentiment: —

"Old Bridgewater, — daughter of Duxbury and granddaughter of Plymouth, — the date of her birth nearly co-eval with her parents. In wealth and population she has excelled them both; and, though cut into four parts, she is as vigorous and fruitful as ever. Her sires, though far behind her, rejoice in her prosperity, and wish you a thousand times as many as ye are."

---

14. " *The Memory of James Keith*, — the first minister ordained in Bridgewater. We are this day enjoying the fruits of his devotedness to the cause of *civil* and *religious liberty*."

Hon. JAMES M. KEITH, of Roxbury, responded as follows: —

MR. PRESIDENT, LADIES AND GENTLEMEN, — A sentiment in memory of the honored dead is generally received standing and in silence; and such a reception, in the present case, would be, I apprehend, a far more eloquent tribute than any I can hope to offer. Indeed, the vocation of one practised in the strife of the forum is little calculated to make him a fitting exponent of the virtues of him who ministers at the shrines of the temple. And yet there is a beauty and moral sublimity in the patient devotion to duty, manifested in the daily life of the conscientious Christian minister, which appeals even to what some consider the callous heart of the legal advocate, in tones more thrilling than the highest-wrought periods uttered from the rostrum.

The eloquence of such a life was shown by the Rev. James Keith, the first minister of Bridgewater, for more than fifty-five years, amidst the toils, the privations, and the dangers of a colonial settlement, in the forests around the spot on which we are assembled. Born in Scotland, educated at Aberdeen, coming to these shores in 1662, ordained in 1664, he continued in the faithful discharge of the duties of his ministry till called to his reward in 1719. He showed his appreciation of "Heaven's last, best gift to man," by an early marriage. He had six sons and three daughters; and his descendants, to the number of more than a thousand, are now found scattered through the New-England States, New York, Michigan, Missouri, and Minnesota; showing that, however his posterity may have failed of obedience to some of the precepts of the Decalogue, they have not forgotten the first command given to man. His descendants have been, so far as I know, an honest, industrious, and law-abiding people. Out of some seven hundred criminal cases reported in the decisions of our Supreme Court, only one is found in which a Keith was a party defendant; and that was a case in which he had been convicted of the illegal sale of intoxicating liquor, on the testimony of a *convicted thief;* and the Court, like sensible men as well as learned judges, set the verdict aside, and thus placed the family name all right upon the record.

The first minister of Bridgewater did not preach, nor did his hearers practise, a sickly sentimentality, which showed more sympathy for the criminal than love for the observance of law; but he taught, and they believed, in a willing obedience to law, and in the speedy punishment of its violators. They devoutly believed in prayer, and trusted in God; but they also trusted in their own right arms to achieve their defence. When attacked by the Indians, whom they had treated with uniform kindness, they did not abandon their homes, as advised by the timid of other settlements, nor trembling wait for Omnipotence specially to interpose for their deliverance; but, seizing their weapons with resolute hearts, they attacked the foe, and drove him from their settlement.

Judging the present inhabitants of Bridgewater by their past history, one could wish that the plains of Kansas were now filled with them; that they might there repel the hordes of violence and oppression, and make those broad savannas vocal with the songs of freemen.

But, at this late hour, I will detain you no longer. I close with this sentiment: —

"Civil and religious liberty, — the priceless inheritance left us by our fathers, which must be maintained at all hazards, and transmitted unimpaired to our children."

---

15. "*Woman.* — She guides the steps of childhood, cheers the labors of *manhood*, and smooths the pillow of age. To her we offer the warmest sentiments of *gratitude* and *love.*"

16. "*The Poet of the Day.* — His subject has inspired his Muse; and we have listened with delight to the words of her inspiration."

Mr. REED, in reply, said, Our friend Governor Washburn had remarked that he never felt more at home in his life; but he (Mr. Reed) must confess that he never felt less so, surrounded as he was by reverend men of all professions. He then gave, as a toast, —

"The descendants of Mrs. Judith Shaw (*to whose memory respectful allusion had been made at the table*), — the best proofs of her piety and frugality."

---

17. "*The Memory of Massasoit,* — the friendly sachem, who sold the township of Bridgewater."

A representative of the Pokanoket tribe made the following response: —

BROTHERS, — I have come a long way to meet you. I am glad that our good old father Massasoit still lives in your memory. These fields were once the hunting-grounds of the red men; but they were sold to the white men of

Bridgewater. The red men have been driven towards the great water at the West, and have disappeared like the dew; while the white men have become like the leaves on the trees, and the sands on the sea-shore.

Brothers, our hunting-grounds grow narrow; the chase grows short; the sun grows low; and, before another Centennial Celebration of the Incorporation of Bridgewater, our bones will be mingled with the dust.

Brothers, may we live in peace! and may the Great Spirit bless the red men and the white men!

---

18. "*The next Centennial Anniversary.* — May it find the doors of the old homestead wide open to receive its returning children; its inmates contented, prosperous, and happy; and our country at *peace, united, and free!*"

By WILLIAM ALLEN: —

"*Bridgewater*, Somersetshire, Old England. — Our friend and correspondent: God bless her! She was the first in all the British empire to send a petition to Parliament for the extirpation of the slave-trade. May neither she, nor her namesake in Massachusetts, cease her efforts in the cause of truth till all humanity is free!"

A sentiment complimentary to Senator SUMNER was offered, and responded to by Rev. PAUL COUCH, of North Bridgewater.

A scroll, of which the following is a copy, was circulated in the tent for signatures: —

"Other men labored; and ye are entered into their labors." — St. John, iv. 38.

"We who have assembled this day to commemorate the Two Hundredth Anniversary of the Incorporation of the Town of Bridgewater, in grateful remembrance of the toils and sufferings of our ancestors, and in the hope that the inheritance they bequeathed to us may be guarded and enjoyed by their descendants to remotest generations, here record our names.

"WEST BRIDGEWATER, Mass., June 3, 1856."

The following Songs, by Mr. D. W. C. PACKARD, of North Bridgewater, were prepared to be sung at the table, but were omitted for the want of time: —

> The glorious band, that brave old band,
> Of honest heart and strong right hand, —
> Oh! noble were the deeds they dared;
> And beauteous, who their danger shared.
> Their hallowed dust our hillsides hold,
> Our valleys bloom above their mould;
> But their spirit lives in our souls to-day:
> It lives — it lives — shall live alway.

> They found these fields when the wolf was here;
> When through the thicket leaped the deer;
> When the Indian's council-fires were red,
> And these peaceful vales with blood were fed.
> The Indian's hard-fought fields are o'er,
> And his council-fires are seen no more;
> But our fathers' spirit it lives to-day:
> It lives — it lives — shall live alway.

> For Freedom was their life-blood given;
> In that dear cause they kneeled to Heaven;
> And Freedom, from the dust they trod,
> Springs up like verdure from the sod.

Their hallowed dust our hillsides hold,
Our valleys bloom above their mould;
But their spirit lives in our souls to-day:
It lives — it lives — shall live alway.

From north, from south, from east, from west,
We come, the sacred spot to bless,
Where first our fathers' anthems broke
The silence of the wilderness.

The place, the time, those honored forms,
Alike our recollection claim;
And, like the dove, she hastens back
To brood o'er each remembered name.

And she shall dress their grassy graves
With wreaths of amaranthine flowers,
And, weeping there, shall smiling turn
To view the blessings that are ours.

And long as waves the golden grain
Above the plains their hands have tilled,
So long as summer fields are green,
Shall memory's cup to them be filled.

More sentiments and songs had been prepared for the occasion; but the end of the centennial day drew near, and they were omitted.

"Union, peace, and joy had crowned that festive day," —

when a vote was passed to adjourn to the next Centennial Anniversary.

LETTERS.

The following letters, among others, were received from gentlemen who had been invited to attend the celebration, but were not read, for want of time: —

From His Excellency Henry J. Gardner.

Boston, May 29, 1856.

My dear Sir, — I have delayed till to-day my reply to the Committee of Invitation for "the Second Centennial Anniversary of the Incorporation of the ancient Town of Bridgewater," in hopes that my official duties would permit me to be present on so interesting an occasion; but present appearances, as well as ascertained engagements, will, beyond a question, deprive me of that pleasure.

Since the day that Capt. Miles Standish purchased of the Indians the territory of your town, for a miscellaneous collection of coats, hatchets, hoes, knives, and moose-skins, it has had historic associations connected with its progress, interesting alike to the antiquarian and the general reader.

My purpose, however, now, is not to attempt writing a new "Bridgewater Treatise," but to express my sincere regrets at my inability to be present on the 3d of June next.

I remain, very respectfully,
  You friend and fellow-citizen,
    Henry J. Gardner.

Austin Packard, Esq., West Bridgewater.

From Hon. Edward Everett.

BOSTON, May 7, 1856.

DEAR SIR, — I have your favor of the 5th, inviting me, on behalf of the Committee appointed for the purpose, to attend the celebration of the Second Centennial Anniversary of the Incorporation of the ancient Town of Bridgewater, on the 3d of June.

I am much indebted to the Committee for the honor of this invitation. Few towns in Massachusetts are of greater importance than Bridgewater in the early history of the Old Colony, or afford ampler subjects for commemoration at the present day. I should have the greatest pleasure, if I were able, in being present on an occasion of so much interest, and particularly in listening to an address from the eminent gentleman who is to speak to you. Other engagements, I regret to say, put it wholly out of my power.

With the best wishes for an agreeable celebration,

I remain, dear sir,

Respectfully yours,

EDWARD EVERETT.

Mr. AUSTIN PACKARD.

From Hon. Charles E. Forbes.

NORTHAMPTON, May 15, 1856.

MY DEAR SIR, — I have received your invitation to be present at the celebration of the Second Centennial Anniversary of the Incorporation of Bridgewater, on the third day of June next. Though born in your ancient and respectable town, my removal from it took place at so early a period in life, that I have no recollection of the event. But, from the conversations of others, I became, during my childhood and youth, very familiar with the names and characters of many of its inhabitants then living; the greater part of whom, in the ordinary course of nature, are now gathered to the fathers. But many of their descendants, of those who bear their names and inherit their virtues, will be present, with whom it would give me great pleasure to unite in the proposed celebration. My engagements, however, will compel me to forego this pleasure; but I beg you to be assured of the sympathy and kind feelings which I shall ever cherish towards the inhabitants of my native town, and towards the descendants of its former inhabitants, in whatever part of the world their destiny may have placed them. Accept for yourself, and be kind enough to convey to the Committee, my thanks for this honor.

I am, very respectfully,
Your obedient servant,
CHARLES E. FORBES.

AUSTIN PACKARD, Esq.

From Hon. Israel Washburn, jun., of Maine.

HOUSE OF REPRESENTATIVES, Washington, May 9, 1856.

DEAR SIR, — I have the honor to acknowledge the receipt of your invitation to be present at the celebration, on the third day of June next, of the Second Centennial Anniversary of the Incorporation of the ancient Town of Bridgewater.

I should rejoice exceedingly to be at this "gathering of the sons and daughters of the four towns:" for there I should meet my relations, and be at home; and there I should have an opportunity to hear the eloquent words of the distinguished gentleman who does so much honor to the name found oftener than any other in the records of Bridgewater. But my duties and engagements here will constrain me to forego this pleasure.

Respectfully, your obedient servant,
I. WASHBURN, jun.

AUSTIN PACKARD, Esq., for the Committee, &c.

From Hon. Elijah Hayward.

McConnelsville, Ohio, May 26, 1856.

Dear Sir, — I have received, and read with much pleasure, your letter of the 5th instant, inviting me to be present, on the 3d of June next, at "the Second Centennial Anniversary of the Incorporation of the ancient Town of Bridgewater;" for which I tender to you, and to the Committee of which you are the organ, my sincere thanks. A temporary illness of the last three weeks has prevented me from earlier making my acknowledgments. It would afford me inexpressible satisfaction to be present at that time, and to participate in the flow of feeling which must then be exhibited, and that love of ancestral pride which belongs to the instincts of our nature; but my previous engagements, which cannot be dispensed with, will, I regret to say, deprive me of that pleasure.

Being a native of the town, "and to the manor born" in 1786, and a lineal descendant of at least nine of its original proprietors and early settlers, — of which your own ancestor, Samuel Packard, was one, — it is impossible for me to be indifferent to those impulses which must be manifested on that great occasion, and to those affectionate reminiscences which add pleasure to the recollections of by-gone events. We view the past in the sepulchres of the generations that have lived before us; we see the present in the conflict of human reason and the human passions; and we contemplate the unseen future in humility, as in the will of the great Creator, to whom alone all time and all knowledge is present. There is not probably a square mile of the original eight miles square, of the ancient territory of Bridgewater, in which there has not been preserved some reminiscent of the first and early fathers of the town, worthy the cherished veneration of their descendants.

The motives which ennoble our nature, and the virtues which adorn the character of mankind, in which no taint of vice ever intermingled, were most happily illustrated in the lives of the first and early settlers of Bridgewater, whose example, now fixed on high, presents a spectacle of virtue, piety, and patriotism, worthy of the most lasting commemoration. We should violate the best feelings of filial affection and gratitude, if we did not most fully appreciate the resulting consequences of their motives and conduct.

But there is another sentiment which must inevitably interpose itself upon the occasion. Many natives of the town, who have long been absent, will then be present, with sensations of another character. There is no feeling more pure, more chaste, than that which is inspired by the multitude of the recollections of the place of our birth, and the scenes of our childhood, connected with the virtues of our ancestors. The clime of our birth, the place where we first experienced the sensations of pleasure, and even those of pain, — "that mysterious attraction which draws us so gently to the first objects of our views and to the earliest of our acquaintance," — possess a secret spell of enchanting reflection, a charm which time sanctifies to our fondest recollections. Even the rude, unlettered savage, — "whose home is the forest, and whose habitation is the shade," — an alien to many of the ordinary feelings and sentiments of humanity, venerates the sepulchres of his fathers, and esteems his birthplace holy ground. It is the triumph of nature, true to its social instincts, over the most violent passions, and all the artifices and refinements of civilization.

What, then, must have been the emotions of those female Pilgrims, the mothers of Bridgewater, when they bade their last adieu to the home of their fathers, the land of their birth, and to all the delicate and bright hopes of their youth! What pious fortitude, what religious zeal, what strong affections, what firmness of purpose, and what serene calmness, must have set enthroned in their bosoms, to have enabled them to forego so much, and to encounter so much, for Christian liberty and social peace! Wonderful women! daughters of a foreign land! mothers of a new generation of heroes, statesmen, and patriots! — your descendants — a free people, a nation prosperous and happy — cherish the recollection of your exalted virtues, and have consecrated them to your memories.

I would, if it were proper, present to the consideration of those assembled on the occasion the following sentiment : —

"*The first and early Fathers of ancient Bridgewater.* — Their lineal descendants honor themselves by doing honor to their memory."

And I would also present the following : —

" *The Mothers and Matrons of the original Town.* — While they taught their offspring the love and the value of civil and religious liberty, they were ever themselves tenacious of the liberty of loving."

With great respect, your obedient servant,

ELIJAH HAYWARD.

AUSTIN PACKARD, Esq., West Bridgewater, Mass.

From Hon. James Savage.

To the Committee for the Centennial Celebration
at West Bridgewater, on 3d June next.   BOSTON, May 16, 1856.

GENTLEMEN, — Very great pleasure should I have in being present at the re-union of ancient Bridgewater, in its fourfold strength, on the recurrence of its natal day for the two hundredth time; and great is the attraction that must reach widely around from the fact that an appropriate address will be delivered by my friend Governor Washburn. Yet my situation forbids me to indulge the hope of partaking in your solemnities, as, on that day, I must be in a distant part of the country; and nothing is permitted me but to express most grateful acknowledgment for your polite invitation. Private friendships would be refreshed by meeting such honored old associates as William Baylies and Artemas Hale; but the advanced years have done much towards making the grasshopper a burden, and leaving little hope of being endured in his garrulity by

Your most obliged,

JAS. SAVAGE.

AUSTIN PACKARD, Esq.

From Hon. C. C. Washburn, of Wisconsin.

WASHINGTON, D.C., May 17, 1856.

MY DEAR SIR, — It would give me great pleasure to accept your polite invitation to be present at the Second Centennial Celebration of the Incorporation of the ancient Town of Bridgewater; but my engagements here are of such a character as to preclude me from doing so; which I much regret. Hoping that you may have a pleasant time,

I am, very truly,

C. C. WASHBURN.

AUSTIN PACKARD, Esq., West Bridgewater, Mass.

ADDRESS

TO THOSE WHO MAY CELEBRATE THE THIRD CENTENNIAL ANNIVERSARY OF THE INCORPORATION OF BRIDGEWATER.

PREPARED BY THE COMMITTEE APPOINTED FOR THAT PURPOSE.

ON the third day of last month, the present inhabitants of our old and favored town met to commemorate the virtues of a peculiar people, the founders of a free and happy community, — our forefathers. This is undoubtedly the first instance in which a centennial celebration of the town has been held. A hundred years ago, the inhabitants of the colonies were so absorbed in the contest at that time raging between the mother country and the colonies on the one side, and the French and Indians on the other, that little time could be spared, and little money expended, for such festivities.

It would be to us highly gratifying, could some memorial of a like day of thanksgiving, held a hundred years ago, now greet our eyes. Pleasant would it be to see the names of those who might have been the actors in such a day of rejoicing; to read a recital of their impressions of the past, their condition in the then present, and their hopes and anticipations of the future; and especially if they had prepared, for transmission to us, their expressions of interest in those, who, at this date, have arisen to fill their places.

No such memorial can be found; but we, from the sympathies of our nature, judging that, to those who shall be here one hundred years hence, a word of congratulation must be welcome, will with pleasure speak to-day to those, who, on the third day of June, 1956, may meet to rejoice over the past; who, in speaking of the men of ancient time, will look back upon us, we hope, as a part of an honored line of ancestry.

As we glance at the past, and then turn to the future, a multitude of thoughts press upon the mind; and the first thought is expressed in the question, If the change in the future be as great as that in the past, what will be the condition of the inhabitants of New England a hundred years hence?

Favored, indeed, has been our community, in common with our nation. When, in the course of the century just closed, our fathers were oppressed, and their cry rose to Heaven for help, God heard their supplications, and brought them deliverance. To an impoverishing and deadly strife succeeded the comforts of peace. The inventive faculty of man has here found ample scope. All the elements of the material world have been taxed to aid in the advancement of America. Inventions and discoveries have been presented to view, astonishing even to ourselves. It is within a very brief period that lightning has become the messenger of thought; and information is transmitted through our country, as it were in a moment, from centre to circumference. The sun, with mathematical precision, performs the office of the landscape or portrait painter; while the researches of science have, by the use of chloroform, rendered surgical operations painless.

Precisely forty-nine years have passed since the first application of steam to navigation in this country, and a little more than a quarter of a century since it was first applied to land carriages. This powerful agent, the steam-engine, — the very " king of machines;" superseding, in a great measure, the former cumbrous methods of locomotion, and daily applied more and more to the promotion of the various branches of art, — is revolutionizing the country. Its future results it is impossible to conceive.

Within the last fifteen years, the friends of education have been making unusual efforts, and we trust with a good degree of success, to discover the best means of educating the youth of our country. Intense activity is the great characteristic of our community. The care-worn countenance and toil-hardened hand, the hum of peaceful industry, and the reverence for things divine, evince the causes of the productive fields of our rural districts, and the wealth of our cities. A prosperity unexampled in the history of any earlier nation has attended ours; and well may the language of the ancient prophet be applied to us, "What could have been done more to my vineyard that I have not done?"

But, notwithstanding the prosperity of the community, it must be regretted that the morals of the people have not fully kept pace with their privileges. The ordinances of divine worship do not, from a part of the people, receive that hearty support which the spiritual wants of our nature demand. A portion, on the sabbath, absent themselves from the house of God. While very few openly oppose religious institutions, too many treat the subject with indifference or lukewarmness.

The cause of temperance, which has suffered ever since the first century of our existence as a town, still meets with obstacles to its success. Men of wealth and influence do not always, in this matter, come with that hearty determination to aid in the exaltation of our community which every true patriot must devoutly desire. For the promotion of this cause, temperance societies have been organized by individuals pledging themselves neither to use ardent spirits as a beverage, nor to encourage others in the use or sale of them. We are gratified to remember, and it may interest you to know, that one of the first of these in the United States was

CENTENNIAL CELEBRATION.   153

the "Bridgewater Temperance Society," formed about forty years ago.

At this moment, a deep excitement pervades our country in relation to the subject of human slavery. Liberty of speech, and the "inalienable right to life, liberty, and the pursuit of happiness," are by many openly denied; and Kansas, the very territorial centre of our Union, is now the great battle-field between justice and oppression. The question now is, Shall Freedom, with its attendant train of blessings, smile upon those lovely fields, and thereafter upon the as yet unsettled parts of our national domain; or shall Slavery, with its legions of iniquities, blast the fair face of nature, and struggle to reach the summit of glory, unheeding the consequent tears, groans, and degradation of multitudes made in the image of God?

For several years past, great efforts have been made to settle difficulties between nations by arbitration. Peace societies, and a convention of representatives from various civilized nations, have striven to hasten the reign of the Prince of Peace throughout the world. Disputes between nations, that, half a century ago, would have ended in the horrors of exterminating war, have, by such means, been amicably settled; though the heart sickens to think of the dreadful woes inflicted by man upon his brother man, in the war just ended between Russia and the combined armies of England, France, and Turkey.

The sabbath school, an institution established among us almost within the past generation, has been the means of great good in our immediate community, as well as throughout our country, and many parts of the civilized world.

Till within a recent period, the ancient township of Bridgewater continued under but one corporation. The large extent of territory induced our people, for greater convenience in municipal matters, to divide, in a friendly spirit, into four sister towns, each retaining Bridgewater as a part of its name.

We are still one in feeling, and rejoice in the good old name of Bridgewater. May the name of each remain unchanged so long as the Pilgrim stock shall last! Like a watch-tower, may it ever diffuse the living flame of devotion to truth and duty!

As we with reverence now pass the old churchyards where "the rude forefathers of our hamlets sleep," so when, after the lapse of another century, you will, in the cemeteries on the shady hillsides of this our old home, gently pass by the moss-covered tablets indicating our last earthly resting-place, and as you decipher the names of the present actors in the drama of life, may you also read on the tablet of the heart the records of many lives that were " long because they answered life's great end"! While you will look back with a smile upon the foibles and unmeaning fashions of the present day, but with respect upon all efforts to reach a higher state of cultivation, moral and intellectual, may you realize, that, while customs change, Christian principle is ever the same, — that none " ever hardened himself against God, and prospered"!

As we are writing these lines on this, the great anniversary of our national independence, the notes of rejoicing at the good fortunes of the land, borne on each passing breeze, bring to mind the fact, that these municipalities are but parts of a stupendous whole; that the weal or woe of one portion tends materially to affect that of all the rest.

The mightiest of questions are now presented to the individual and national conscience, surpassing any that have arisen within the memory of living men.

To the welfare of yourselves and your successors, we look with a solicitude we cannot express. In infinite wisdom, the Father of all the generations of man has concealed the future from our view. As on the tempestuous sea of life the bark shall sail freighted with the destinies of this people, may that great chart which guided the Pilgrim Fathers ever teach you to avoid the rocks and shoals on which so many nations have foundered! And that righteousness which alone exalts both individuals and nations, as it blessed our fathers, so may it bless our descendants through all future ages!

WILLIAM ALLEN.
PAUL COUCH.
JOSEPH KINGMAN.
EDWARD SOUTHWORTH, jun.
THOMAS CUSHMAN.
ASA MITCHELL.
DWELLEY FOBES.

EAST BRIDGEWATER, July 4, 1856.

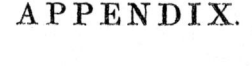

APPENDIX.

"A MUSTER-ROLL OF THE COMPANY UNDER THE COMMAND OF CAPT. THOMAS MITCHELL (BELONGING TO THE REGIMENT WHEREOF THOMAS CLAPP, ESQ., IS COLONEL), THAT MARCHED, ON THE ALARM FOR THE RELIEF OF FORT WILLIAM-HENRY, IN AUGUST, 1757." *

Daniel Pettingal.	George Harris.	Josiah Mahurin.
Beriah Willis.	Joshua Willis, jun.	William Barlow.
John Bolton.	Perez Waterman, jun.	Amos Hayward.
Thomas Carr.	James Snow.	Joseph Harvey.
Robert Ripley.	Jonas Turner.	Isaac Lee.
Benjamin Munk.	John Doughty.	Jonathan Pratt.
Daniel Littlefield.	Robert Leach.	Josiah Leach.
Jonathan Randall.	Henry Chamberlain.	Moses Sash.
John Loring.	Jonathan Willis.	Matthew Buck.
James Allen.	Benjamin Mahurin.	Joseph Belcher.
Eliphalet Cary.	Henry Washburn.	George Packard.
Timothy Hayward.	Joseph Keith.	Francis Goward.
Edward Packard.	Stephen Leach.	Hezekiah Mahurin.
Elisha Hooper.	Eliab Washburn.	Timothy Fobes.
Robert Gilmore.	David Perkins, jun.	Samuel Packard, jun.
Joseph Samson.	Uriah Richard.	Gregory Belcher.
Ephraim Allen.	Abisha Leach.	Ebenezer Edson.

* The original "Roll" is now in an almost perfect state of preservation. — June 3, 1856.

The following is copied from "Boston News-Letter," Oct. 21, 1773: —

"BRIDGEWATER, Oct. 13, 1773.

"Col. Edson's Regiment, consisting of nine foot-companies of this Town and two of Abington, was reviewed this day by his Excellency the Governor (Hutchinson). His Excellency was met at the entrance of the Town by a number of the principal inhabitants, and conducted to the house of the Rev. Mr. Angier (John), near the place of parade. There were about seven hundred men in arms, and a greater concourse of people than has been known to have been in the Town upon any other occasion."

The Review was on the "Common" at East Bridgewater. The Rev. John Angier owned and occupied the place now owned and occupied by James H. Mitchell, Esq., of East Bridgewater.

"MUSTER-ROLL OF THE LATE CAPT. JACOB ALLEN'S* COMPANY OF THE FIRST MASSACHUSETTS REGIMENT OF FOOT IN THE SERVICE OF THE UNITED STATES, COMMANDED BY COL. JOHN BAILEY; TAKEN FOR THE MONTH OF FEBRUARY, 1778."

COMMISSIONED.

Jan. 1, 1777 . . . . JONATHAN ALLEN, *First Lieutenant.*
   ,,   ,, ... JOTHAN AMES, *Second Lieutenant.*
   ,,   ,, ... ROTHEAS MITCHELL, *Ensign.*

Sergeants.
1. Amos Harden.†
2. Watson Babington.
3. William Latham.

Corporals.
1. Daniel Ramsdill.
2. Caleb Howard.
3. Solomon Conant.

Drum and Fife.
1. Eliphaz Mitchell.

Privates.
1. John Bolton.
2. ——— ‡
3. John Clapp.
4. Lot Dwelley.
5. Boatswain Duel.
6. Richard Farrington.
7. James Welch.
8. William Parsons.
9. Prince Hall.
10. March Lewis.
11. Thomas Latham.
12. William Fowller.
13. Reuben Mitchell.
14. Jonathan Mehurin.
15. William Mattris.
16. Robert Robinson.
17. Isaac Houghton.
18. Peleg Pendill.
19. David Poor.
20. James Robinson, jr.
21. William Robbins.
22. Henry Richmond.
23. Rufus Robbins.
24. Enoch Stocken.
25. Enos Whitman.
26. Japhet Allen.
27. Elisha Curtis.
28. Brister Drake.
29. Michael Fitzgerald.
30. Silas Harris.
31. Abraham Perkins.
32. John Lope.
33. Micha White.
34. John Wilkens.
35. James Ramsdill.
36. Sippeo Solomon.
37. Joseph Semore.
38. ——— ‡ Wood.

RELIGIOUS SOCIETIES.

WEST BRIDGEWATER.

First Congregational, Unitarian, founded 1656. No settled minister.
Baptist . . . Cochesett Village, founded 1781. No settled minister.
Meth.-Epis., Cochesett Village, founded 1840. Rev. Edward B. Hinckley, Pastor.
New Jerusalem . . . . founded 1847. No settled minister.

---

* Killed at the Battle of Stillwater, Sept. 19, 1777.
† Killed at Kingsbridge, N. Y., July, 1781.   ‡ Name lost.

APPENDIX. 161

BRIDGEWATER.

First Congregational, Unitarian .	established 1716.	Rev. John J. Putnam, Pastor.
Congregational, Trinitarian . . .	established 1822.	Rev. David Brigham, Pastor.
Cong., Trin., Scotland Village . .	established 1833.	Rev. Otis Rockwood, Pastor.
Episcopal	founded 1747.	No settled clergyman.
New Jerusalem	founded 1833.	Rev. Thos. P. Rodman, Pastor.
Catholic	House erected 1855.	Rev. A. L. Roache, Pastor.

EAST BRIDGEWATER.

First Congregational, Unitarian . .	founded 1723.	Rev. Joseph H. Phipps, Pastor.
Union Society of E. & W. Bridgew.	founded 1826.	Rev. Philo B. Wilcox, Pastor.
Trinitarian Congregational	founded 1849.	Rev. Baalis Sanford, Pastor.
New Jerusalem	founded 1834.	Rev. Timothy O. Paine, Pastor.
Universalist	founded 1834.	No settled clergyman.
Methodist-Episcopal	founded 1850.	Rev. Eli Strobridge.

NORTH BRIDGEWATER.

First Congregational, Trinitarian .	founded 1738.	Rev. Paul Couch, Pastor.
South Cong., Trin., Campello Vill.,	founded 1837.	Rev. David T. Packard, Pastor.
Porter Church, Trinitarian Cong.,	founded 1850.	Rev. Charles L. Mills, Pastor.
New Jerusalem	founded 1827.	Rev. Warren Goddard, Pastor.
First Meth.-Epis. (West Shares) . .	founded 1830.	Rev. A. B. Wheeler, Pastor.
Second Methodist-Episcopal	founded 1851.	Rev. Robt. McGonnegal, Pastor.
Baptist	founded 1850.	No settled clergyman.
Catholic	founded 1853.	Rev. A. L. Roache, Pastor.

CENSUS OF 1855.

	West Bridgewater.	Bridgewater.	East Bridgewater.	North Bridgewater.	Total.
Population	1,734	3,363*	2,930	5,208	13,235
Americans	1,462	2,777	2,633	4,307	11,179
Foreigners	272	577	297	901	2,047
Unknown	. . .	9	. . .	. . .	9
Under 10	434	820	477	1,240	2,971
10 to 20	345	610	564	1,080	2,549
20 to 30	311	585	574	1,123	2,593
30 to 40	243	430	409	790	1,872
40 to 50	159	343	259	451	1,212
50 to 60	108	236	231	298	873
60 to 70	80	184	158	170	592
70 to 80	36	108	53	71	268
80 to 90	18	30	19	15	82
90 to 100	. . .	4	. . .	2	6
Age not stated . . .	. . .	13	6	18	37
No. Families . . .	354	609	700	1,171	2,834
No. Dwelling Houses	301	539	581	979	2,400
No. Polls	437	750	810	1,425	3,422
Births	68	89	100	202	459
Deaths	31	41	30	88	190
Valuation	$652,880.00	$1,822,426.00	$1,206,940.00	$1,925,378.66	$5,607,624.66
Whole Tax	4,373.25	9,246.71	8,819.69	13,744.12	36,183.77
Raised for Com. Schools	1,200.00	2,500.00	2,500.00	3,500.00	9,700.00
Square miles . . .	16¾	28 1-6	18 1-7	19½	82 1-56

* Exclusive of 441 inmates of State Almshouse, the population is 2,922.

STATISTICS OF INDUSTRY IN 1855.

WEST BRIDGEWATER.

Furnaces for m. of hollow ware and castings, 4; hollow ware and other castings m'd., 295 tons ; val. of hollow ware and castings, $16,900 ; cap., $21,000; emp., 29.

Manufactories of shovels and spades, 1 (partly m'd. in this town, and finished in Easton); cap., $10,000; emp., 9.

Establishments for m. of wagons, sleighs, and other vehicles, 4; val. of wagons, &c., m'd., $4,680; cap., $1,800; emp., 8.

Cabinet manufactories, 1 ; val. of chairs and cabinet ware, $1,000 ; cap., $200; emp., 3.

Boots of all kinds m'd., 27,600 pairs; shoes of all kinds m'd., 141,700 pairs; val. of boots and shoes, $178,460; m. emp., 204; f. emp., 96.

Val. of straw braid m'd., and not made into bonnets and hats, $383,95; f. emp., 24.

Charcoal m'd., 6,840 bush.; val. of same, $1,018.60; emp., 4.

Lumber prepared for market, 189,833 ft.; val. of lumber, $2,970.50; emp., 35, part of the time.

Firewood prepared for market, 985 cords; val. of firewood, $4,633,50; emp., 57, part of the time.

Sheep, 11; val. of all sheep, $33; wool produced, 61 lbs.

Horses, 144; val. of horses, $9,194. Oxen, over three years old, 151; steers, under three years old, 21; val. of oxen and steers, $8,821. Milch cows, 347; heifers, 63; val. of cows and heifers, $13,346.

Butter, 20,588 lbs.; val. of butter, $5,147. Cheese, 5,590 lbs.; val. of cheese, $698.75.

Honey, 174 lbs; val. of honey, $35.34.

Indian corn, 192 acres; Indian corn, per acre, 28 bush.; val., $5,386.

Wheat, 3 acres; wheat, per acre, 16⅔ bush.; val., $125.

Rye, 28 acres; rye, per acre, 15½ bush; val., $666.

Barley, 9 acres; barley, per acre, 19 8-9 bush.; val., $179.

Oats, 55 acres; oats, per acre, 22 7-55 bush.; val., $791.05.

Potatoes, 133 acres; potatoes, per acre, 87 bush.; val., $8,703.

Beets, and other esculent vegetables, 8 acres; val., $690.

English mowing, 953½ acres; English hay, 844¾ tons; val., $16,995.

Wet-meadow or swale hay, 858 tons; val., $8,580.

Apple-trees, 7,980; val. of apples, $3,424.50.

Pear-trees, 356; val. of pears, $53.75.

Cranberries, 86 acres; val., $969.35.

Beeswax, 3 lb; val., $1.

Establishments for m. of boot and shoe boxes, 1; cap., $3,000; val. of boxes m'd., $4,000; emp., 3.

Val. of vanes m'd., $4,000; cap., $1,500; emp., 3.

Onions, turnips, carrot, and beets raised, 1,380 bush.; val., $690.

APPENDIX.

BRIDGEWATER.

Rolling, slitting, and nail mills, 4; iron m'd., and not made into nails, 1,000 tons; val. of iron, $80,000; machines for m. of nails, 52; nails m'd., 62,500 casks; val. of nails, $250,000; cap., $77,000; emp., 207.
Forges, 2; iron m'd., 70 tons; val. of iron, &c., $10,500; cap., $6,000; emp., 20.
Furnaces for m. of hollow ware and castings, 1; hollow ware and other castings m'd., 600 tons; val. of hollow ware, &c., $40,000; cap., $18,000; emp., 30.
Paper manufactories, 2; stock made use of, 270 tons; paper m'd., 210 tons; val. of paper, $30,000; cap., $18,000; emp., 20.
Establishments for m. of chaises, wagons, sleighs, and other vehicles, 2; val. of vehicles m'd., $5,800; cap., $2,000; emp., 7.
Establishment for m. of soap, 2; soap m'd., 25,120 gals; val. of soap, $2,540; cap., $1,500; emp., 3.
Tin-ware manufactories, 1; val. of tin ware, $500; cap., $500; emp., 2.
Establishments for m. of cotton gins, 1; val. of cotton gins m'd., $14,000; cap., $30,000; emp., 40.
Boots of all kinds m'd., 600 pairs; shoes of all kinds m'd., 166,000 pairs; val. of boots and shoes, $125,700; m. emp., 55; f. emp., 35.
Bricks m'd., 3,000,000; val. of bricks, $12,000; emp., 30.
Charcoal m'd., 63,600 bush; val. of same, $4,000; emp., 20.
Lumber prepared for market, 900,000 ft.; val. of lumber, $7,600; emp., 30.
Firewood prepared for market, 2,217 cords; val. of firewood, $6,651; emp., 30.
Horses, 229; val. of horses, $16,472. Oxen, over three years old, 151; steers, under three years old, 18; value of oxen and steers, $7,557. Milch cows, 444; heifers, 51; val. of cows and heifers, $14,228.
Butter, 25,836 lbs; val. of butter, $6,459. Cheese, 6,670 lbs; val. of cheese, $834; Honey, 130 lbs; val. of honey, $26.
Indian corn, 283 acres; Indian corn, per acre, 29 bush.; val., $8,136.
Wheat, 1½ acre; wheat, per acre, 16 bush.; val., $48.
Rye, 57 acres; rye, per acre, 11 bush.; val., $857.
Barley, 3½ acres; barley, per acre, 24 bush.; val., $80.
Oats, 129 acres; oats, per acre, 23 bush.; val., $1,898.
Potatoes, 157 acres; potatoes, per acre, 86 bush.; val., $6,786.
Onions, 1 acre; onions, per acre, 380 bush.; val., $190.
Turnips, cultivated as a field crop, 4½ acres; turnips, per acre, 325 bush.; val., $450.
Carrots, ½ acre; carrots, per acre, 416 bush.; val., $62.
Beets, and other esculent vegetables, ¾ acre; val., $42.
English mowing, 1,540 acres; English hay, 1,128 tons; val., $20,304.
Wet-meadow or swale hay, 414 tons; val., $4,140.
Apple-trees, 9,299; val. of apples, $3,902.
Pear-trees, 1,180; val. of pears, $128.
Cranberries, 14 acres: val., $520.
Establishments for m. of shingle and box-board mills, 1; mills m'd., 12; val., $4,000; cap., $3,000; emp., 5.

EAST BRIDGEWATER.

Rolling, slitting, and nail mills, 1; iron m'd., and not made into nails, 1,000 tons; val. of iron, $70,000; machines for m. of nails, 29; nails m'd., 24,000 kegs; val. of nails, $96,000; cap., $50,000; emp., 75.
Forges, 1; wrought iron m'd., 468 tons; val. of bar iron, &c., $32,760; cap., $2,000; emp., 5.

Furnaces for m. of hollow ware and castings, 1; hollow ware, &c., m'd., 100 tons; val. of hollow ware, &c., $7,000; cap., $8,000; emp., 8.
Establishments for m. of machinery, 1; val., of machinery m'd., $10,000; cap., $8,000; emp., 10.
Establishments for m. of steam-engines, 1; val. of engines, $51,000; cap., $50,000; emp., 35.
Tack and brad manufactories, 2; tacks and brads m'd., 450 tons; val. of tacks and brads, $70,000; cap., $15,000; m. emp., 56; f. emp., 12; no. of tack machines, 76.
Brass foundries, 1; val. of articles m'd., $600; cap., $500; emp., 2.
Saddle, harness, and trunk manufactories, 2; val. of saddles, &c., $2,000; cap., $1,400; emp., 2.
Establishments for m. of boats, 1; boats built, 6; cap., $300; emp., 1.
Establishments for m. of chaises, wagons, sleighs, and other vehicles, 3; val. of vehicles m'd., $4,000; cap., $1,700; emp., 6.
Establishments for m. of firearms, 1; val. of firearms, $1,000; cap., $800; emp., 1.
Tin-ware manufactories, 2; val. of tin ware, $4,000; cap., $1,500; emp., 5.
Establishments for m. of cotton gins, 2; val. of cotton gins m'd., $85,000; cap., $84,000; emp., 60.
Boots of all kinds m'd., 3,120 pairs; shoes of all kinds m'd., 442,200 pairs; val. of boots and shoes, $399,200; m. emp., 235; f. emp., 134.
Bricks m'd., 500,000; val. of bricks, $2,500; emp., 9.
Val. of snuff, tobacco, and cigars, $4,400; m. emp., 5; f. emp., 2.
Val. of mechanics' tools m'd., $3,000; emp., 2.
Lumber prepared for market, 608,000 ft.; val. of lumber, $6,530; emp., 21.
Shingles m'd., 379,000; val. of shingles, $947.50.
Firewood prepared for market, 2,175 cords; val. of firewood, $6,990; emp., 7.
Sheep, 11; val. of sheep, $33; wool produced, 36 lbs.
Horses, 214; val. of horses, $19,250. Oxen, over three years old, 104; steers, under three years old, 33; val. of oxen and steers, $6,121. Milch cows, 359; heifers, 63; val. of cows and heifers, $14,246.
Butter, 22,752 lbs.; val. of butter, $6,825.60. Cheese, 4,310 lbs.; val. of cheese, $603.40.
Indian corn, 209¾ acres; Indian corn, per acre, 30 bush.; val., $7,046.48.
Wheat, 3¼ acres; wheat, per acre, 20 bush.; val. $130.
Rye, 33¼ acres; rye, per acre, 20 bush.; val., $997.50.
Barley, 6¾ acres; barley, per acre, 25 bush.; val., $195.41.
Oats, 29¾ acres; oats, per acre, 25 bush.; val., $371.87.
Potatoes, 252½ acres; potatoes, per acre, 100 bush.; val., $25,250.
Turnips, cultivated as a field-crop, 6½ acres; turnips, per acre, 300 bush; value, $780.
Carrots, 4 acres; carrots, per acre, 400 bush.; val., $960.
English mowing, 1,314½ acres; English hay, 728½ tons; val., $14,570.
Wet-meadow or swale hay, 510 tons; val., $5,100.
Apple-trees, 8,042; val. of apples, $1,657.
Pear-trees, 1,021; val. of pears, $173.
Cranberries, 7 acres; val., $250.
Establishments for m. of boxes for packing boots, shoes, tacks, and brads, 2; val. of boxes m'd., $15,450; cap., $9,100; emp., 9.
Establishments for m. of cap tubes, 1; tubes m'd., 4,800,000; val. of tubes, $4,800; cap., $3,000; emp., 3.
Nurseries, 2; val. sold, $2,000; cap., $4,100; emp., 3.
Establishments for m. of patterns, 1; val. of patterns m'd., $2,000; emp., 1.

APPENDIX.

NORTH BRIDGEWATER.

Musical-instrument manufactories, 2; val. of musical instruments m'd., $8,780; cap., $2,000; emp., 9.

Daguerreotype artists, 1; daguerreotypes taken, 800; cap., $450; emp., 1.

Brush manufactories, 2; val. of brushes, $8,000; cap., $3,000; emp., 11.

Saddle, harness, and trunk manufactories, 1; val. of saddles, &c., $6,000; cap., $2,000; emp., 4.

Establishments for m. of chaises, wagons, sleighs, and other vehicles, 3; val. of carriages m'd., $5,200; cap., $1,600; emp., 8.

Establishments for m. of soap and tallow candles, 2; soap m'd., 280 bbls.; val. of soap, $1,120.

Chair and cabinet manufactories, 1; val. of chairs and cabinet ware, $20,000; cap., $10,000; emp., 32.

Tin-ware manufactories, 2; val. of tin ware, $13,000; cap., $4,600; emp., 7.

Boots of all kinds m'd., 66,956 pairs; shoes of all kinds m'd., 694,760 pairs; val., of boots and shoes, $724,847; m. emp., 692; f. emp., 484.

Val. of building stone quarried and prepared for building, $500; emp., 4.

Val. of blacking, $8,000; emp., 4.

Val. of blocks and pumps m'd., $50; emp., 1.

Val. of mechanics' tools m'd., $2,540; emp., 44.

Lasts m'd., 40,000; val., $10,000.

Lumber prepared for market, 213,000 ft.; val. of lumber, $32,025.

Firewood prepared for market, 3,348 cords; val. of firewood, $13,796; emp., 60.

Sheep, 5; val. of sheep, $10; wool produced, 20 lbs.

Horses, 343; val. of horses, $29,880. Oxen, over three years old, 74; steers, under three years old, 26; val. of oxen and steers, $5,760. Milch cows, 420; heifers, 36; val. of cows and heifers, $17,068.

Butter, 20,075 lbs.; val. of butter, $5,018.75. Cheese, 6,505 lbs.; val. of cheese, $650.50. Honey, 620 lbs.; val. of honey, $155.

Indian corn, 216 acres; Indian corn, per acre, 28 bush.; val., $6,075.

Rye, 25 acres; rye, per acre, 15 bush.; val., $567.

Barley, 7 acres; barley, per acre, 23 bush.; val., $240.

Oats, 20 acres; oats, per acre, 19 bush.; val., $225.60.

Potatoes, 310 acres; potatoes, per acre, 90 bush.; val., $27,667.

Turnips, 5 acres; turnips, per acre, 200 bush.; val., $250.

Carrots, ½ acre; carrots, per acre, 400 bush.; val., $50.

Beets, and other esculent vegetables, 20 acres; val., $5,000.

English mowing, 1,550 acres; English hay, 1,266 tons; val., $25,320.

Wet-meadow or swale hay, 375 tons; val., $3,750.

Apple-trees, 7,700; val. of apples, $3,000.

Pear-trees, 818; val. of pears, $100.

Cranberries, 16 acres; val., $3,200.

Beeswax, 100 lbs.; val., $73.

Bakeries, 1; flour consumed, 200 bbls.; val. of bread m'd., $5,000; cap., $4,000; emp., 6.

Establishments for m. of shoe boxes, 1: val. of boxes m'd., $1,500; cap., $1,000; emp., 1.

Val. of boot-trees and forms m'd., $2,000.

Peat, 500 cords; val., $2,000.

Swine raised, 526; val., $4,208.

HOUSES OF WORSHIP AND TOWN-MEETINGS.

The first house of worship, in ancient Bridgewater, was built of logs, about the year 1660. It is supposed to have stood near the site of the dwelling-house now occupied by Mr. Simeon Dunbar, in West Bridgewater.

The second house was erected in 1674, in the square directly opposite where Major Jarvis D. Burrill now lives. The dimensions are noticed in Judge Washburn's Address. The Building Committee were Nicholas Byram, John Washburn, Samuel Allen, John Ames, Deacon John Willis, and Goodman (Samuel) Edson.

The third meeting-house, near the centre of Bridgewater, — a view of which is placed at the beginning of this pamphlet, — was built, in 1731, on the site of the second. The Building Committee were Jonathan Hayward, jun., Israel Packard, Thomas Hayward, 3d, Ephraim Fobes, and Ephraim Hayward. The house was fifty feet long, thirty-eight wide, and twenty-two high, and entirely covered with shingles. Eleven places for pews were sold for one hundred and forty-three pounds ten shillings; and, also, a pew was built, on the left side of the pulpit, for the use of the minister's family. The body of the house was furnished with long seats instead of pews. The edifice was three stories high, with two galleries, one above the other, on three sides.

In 1767, the "balcony" was repaired, and a new spire erected upon it, and provision was made for hanging a bell which was purchased the same year. This was the second bell hung in the town, the North Parish having purchased one in 1764. This building was used as a house of worship for seventy years, till the erection of the fourth house on land bought of Gamaliel Howard, near the orchard of Jonathan Copeland.

In 1802, the West Parish voted to give the town of Bridgewater the old meetinghouse, the third, and the land on which it stood, for the purpose of holding townmeetings, so long as they should keep the house in repair. The belfry was then taken down, and town-meetings were accordingly held in that house till the division of the town in 1822. The building was taken down in 1823, having served the purpose of a town-house ninety years.

The old "Double-Decker" was an object of interest to persons of all ages. It was the great focus of the several parishes; and the exciting debates during the war of 1812, and the amusing incidents connected with the house, are fresh in the minds of many of the older residents among us. Soon after the building began to be used solely as a town-hall, a magazine was built in the north-west corner of the upper gallery; and the ammunition of the town was brought from the "Old Powder House," and stored, to the great delight of the boys, who used to find here ample materials for the manufacture of "plummets," which were to grace their writing-books at the winter school. On the division of the town, the remaining warlike materials were distributed among the four towns.

The Selectmen, for many years previous to the separation, were Mr. John Willis, of the West; Mr. Silvanus Pratt, of the South; Capt. Ezra Kingman, of the East; and Capt. Abel Kingman, of the North.

APPENDIX.

Of the seven Town Clerks, from 1656 to 1822, a period of a hundred and sixty-six years, Capt. Eliakim Howard was the last, having served forty-three years. It was the practice, for a long series of years, after the citizens had assembled in town-meeting, for the Selectmen to deputize two of their number to go to the house of Rev. Dr. Reed, and escort him to the town-house, where the venerable man preceded the business of the day with prayer.

The number assembled was sometimes so great, that it was found almost impossible to declare a vote, on some important question, *within* the house; and the company adjourned to the street, where, after a careful array of lines along the road leading to the north, the yeas taking the east side, and the nays the west, the whole sometimes reaching Mr. Gamaliel Howard's corner, a decision of the question was obtained. The highest number of votes ever cast in the house was nine hundred and six.

Usually, after a town-meeting was over, the proceedings of the day closed with a wrestling match: the Parishes challenging each other, frequently the North and East being arrayed against the West and South.

THE END.